AF244099

# The Ds *of* Life

## How to Turn Them to As and Bs

T. LaCroix

ISBN: 978-0-9989102-4-6

Library of Congress Control Number: 2018956619

Sanders Publications LLC

This book is dedicated to the women, whose voices were silenced, as little girls, for telling their "truths." The little girls who couldn't tell their truths. The little girls who didn't speak up in order to protect someone else.

# Contents


Disappointment.................................................... 15

Damage............................................................ 25

Discouragement.................................................... 45

Distance ......................................................... 65

Deployment ....................................................... 73

Daddy ............................................................ 89

Divide & Degree................................................... 119

Deal-Breakers .................................................... 135

Dead Weight....................................................... 151

Deserve .......................................................... 173

# Acknowledgements

First and foremost, thank you Lord for *allowing* me to be *free* enough to share my journey with others. I am forever grateful that you have *allowed* my voice to be heard around the world. It has always been my prayer that you be well pleased with me.

To my husband, Marcus LaCroix, you are truly God's grace and blessing in my life. Thank you for accepting me "just the way I am" and *allowing* me to spread my wings and soar like the Eagle, God has called me to be. Your commitment, dedication, love, and sleepless nights do not go unnoticed. Thank you and I love you.

To my first seed, William, I am blessed to be your mom. You have always challenged me to be a better person. So, I pray you will be as proud of me, as I am of you.

To my "sista-friend," Shameka, thank you for believing in me, loving me as a "sista-friend," and believing that this book could be greater than I could ever imagine. You are truly special to me. I love you and thank you.

To Elizabeth Wilson, thank you for *seeing* me. More specifically, thank you for loving the adult in me, and *seeing* what God *sees* in me. I love you.

To Khloé, who knew that you being in my belly (when I finished this) would push me to complete the projects I had procrastinated on? If you learn anything from me, I want you to know I lived this journey, so you wouldn't have to. You are Beautiful, Bold, Brilliant, Brave, and have a Billionaire flow. Don't let anyone tell you any different. Seek God always.

Finally, I want to acknowledge the women of color, who suffer in silence, believing that other women are judging them when in reality, they are hurting too.

I wrote this book for you. I want you to know that your voice is important and that there are people, who are waiting for you to speak your "truths" – waiting for you to get to a place of healing, so they can also be healed. So, how about we heal together? I'm ready. Are you?

# *Foreword*

I'm sure you've all heard the phrase "life happens." Well, guess what? Life happens to everyone! No one is an exception. It is a part of 'adulting.' You know the part where you have to make the hard decisions.

Decisions you don't want to or would like to make. Decisions that will benefit your future. Decisions that will force you to make conscious efforts to carry them out. Decisions that will cause other people to talk about you. Decisions that will lead to consequences for both you and your family.

T. LaCroix provides readers with prolific insight on how to make these decisions, and deal with their consequences.

As adults, we try to hide things from the world. We put on a façade as if we are the only ones going through things. As if we have it all together when in reality we don't. But little do we know God uses these moments to help someone else.

In this book, T. Lacroix addresses these moments, from a practical perspective, to help us better understand that God is always true to His word.

As you read, I'm sure you will find something you have faced or can relate to in the pages of this book. As men, women, young men, and young women, we all know there is no rule book or guide to addressing disappointment, discouragements, "daddy issue," "deal-breakers," dead weight, and so many other "D's" of life. But, we must learn how to handle them in healthier ways. Ways that result in inner peace and joy.

Yes, everyone is different, and because of that we interpret and handle situations differently. However, at the end of the day, when you lay your head on your pillow, it is you that has to deal with your issues. So, as you read this book, you will find that T. LaCroix helps you realize your journey is just that..."your journey." And, as a result, you must start living a life that will bring about your inner peace and joy.

Dr. Shameka Mack Sanders

# Disappointment

Disappointment /ˌdisəˈpointmənt/ (Noun) - A feeling of sadness or displeasure caused by the non-fulfillment of one's hopes or expectations.

**LESSON**: "I can only live to please God. I can not expect the same from others."

When I think of the word, "disappointment," the first thing that "pops" in my mind is, "I have been disappointed by *so* many people." My second thought is, "I have disappointed *so* many people." My third thought is, "Where do I go from here?" Let's start with the former.

For those, who have disappointed me in the past, I take full responsibility for *allowing* them to be a disappointment.

It is my investment that has *allowed* others to disappoint me. Therefore, this is ultimately a trust issue. For example, you place your trust in people, believing that they will, in fact, do what they say they will do.

But, if you really think about it, it goes far beyond doing things or completing tasks. When you call someone "sister," "brother," "mother," "friend," "partner," etc., there is an "expectation." And, these individuals know what it takes to perform this very important job.

Yet, when they fall short or "mess up," according to your "expectations," you are understandably disappointed. In this sense, you learn that it is not about the actual situation, rather, it's really about your own lack of emotional control. It is this lack of control that causes *you* to feel disappointed in them.

The amount of time you spend misusing your energy and dealing with the emotional consequences of disappointments - talking about them and *allowing* these disappointments to stir up different emotions in you, this is time wasted. In other words, you *could have* used this time to do something more productive.

The truth is most of my disappointments stem from my family dynamics. You see, I was taught one thing, led to believe another, and then found out the truth after my grandparents passed.

I was being *hoodwinked* and *bamboozled*.

My family sold me a *Willie Wonka* hope and a lollipop dream of what a family *should* be, not necessarily what it actually was – at least not based on what I know now about family. Truth-be-told, the funniest part of this illusion was my own family. Because at the end of the day, one's family is not supposed to be dysfunctional and we were as dysfunctional as they came

So, I believed the dream but saw the lie. *Still*, I couldn't understand how my very own family felt they could steal from me. How they could think they had the right to tell me how to live my life. How they could tell me that love hurts, when in fact, love doesn't hurt, and love doesn't keep track of things.

Love gives but doesn't brag. Love also cheers you on. Because of this, I am at a place in my life, where *I am love*. So, after reflecting on my past experiences with my family, I believe my disappointment stemmed from my concept of family. I was really disappointed with my family members.

Their words were not matching up with their actions. I had been misinformed, and now, I had to re-program my mind to have genuinely productive relationships with other people. Because at the end of the day, what I thought was love was not love.

Now, I know what love really is and isn't. As a result, I no longer *allow* my emotional connection to my family or other individuals, in general, or the lack thereof, to be the cause of my disappointment.

Why not? Well, I'm not disappointed anymore

because I have a clear understanding of what a *real* relationship is. I also realize that I can't "expect" more from others, then they can give or more than what I expect from myself.

For example, you can't expect a two-year-old to drive a *Rolls-Royce*. However, a toddler *may* have the ability to push a toy car.

Thus, I no longer have these "expectations" towards my family members and others. Instead, I simply "appreciate" my *real* relationships.

Bottom line, disappointments are distractions. And, because they are distractions, you *must* take control of them. Don't *allow* disappointments to hurt you. Rather, *allow* yourself to learn and grow from them. *Allow* yourself to be *free* of disappointments, so you can "bounce back" from them. After all, it is the "bounce back" that *forces* you to grow and be fulfilled.

I've also been disappointed in my decisions in the past. But, addressing disappointments in oneself is challenging. The truth is I have become disappointed in the decisions I have made, the places I have gone, and the results I have received.

We all have a moment or moments of disappointment. It is not a question of if it will come, because it will. So, the *real* question is, "How can I 'bounce back' quickly after I have been disappointed?"

## Homework

### *Bounce Back*

My biggest challenge has been learning how to "bounce back" quickly from disappointments. Partly, because my emotional state was not "fully intact." When you emotionally-disconnect from people, things, and situations, you *see* things differently.

It becomes a *choice* to be upset vs. taking control of your emotions. I remember I used to talk about a subject for weeks. I told so many people about my situation, and why I was disappointed. Then, one day, I realized that this was causing me to be more distracted and less productive at home and at work.

When I would later come in contact with the people, places, and things that caused my disappointment, old hurts and memories would re-appear, causing me to experience the disappointment all over again. *As a result, this crazy, emotional roller coaster ride just wouldn't stop!* It didn't take me long to realize I was never going to focus if I kept on this route. *It was then that I realized that one's "bounce back" must include a few things, such as:*

~ The courage to address issues: If you need to address an issue with someone, then do so. Decide if it's really worth stirring things up. If not, move on to something more productive.

~ Learn to disconnect: You may need to "disconnect" from those, who constantly disappoint you. Remove yourself from people and places that have become a disappointment to you. For instance, if every time you go to a certain place, it is full of negative energy, don't go back to it. The same goes for people. If the people you are hanging out with are always negative, "disconnect" from them. You may want to even consider completely disconnecting from these people and places. The thing is, for this to work, you must leave your emotions at the door. Why? Well, because it's important not to allow the things you are going through to shake your stability. These "things" do not have to cause you to behave irrationally. Remember, the "situation" is only temporary.

~ Be clear about your expectations: Many times, I have been disappointed because my "expectations" were not clear. Not only were they not clear, but they also didn't address the *real* issue, when it occurred. Therefore, you must stand your ground, especially when it comes to your "expectations." Also, keep in mind that people are not mind readers. Thus, you can't automatically assume they know how you feel or what you want. That is why clear communication is so important. When you have clear communication and "expectations," you are less likely to be disappointed when your needs aren't met.

### *Appreciate*

When you only have "expectations" in yourself and in the Lord, things go a lot better. It's important to be "appreciative" of the opportunities you are given. With a thankful heart, you can change how you *see* your life and situation.

Do things happen? YES! Do situations arise? YES! Do people neglect to come through? YES! However, when those things happen, it is important that you *still* be "appreciative" for the good things in your life.

Remember, *disappointments are only temporary* unless you *allow* the situation to last longer than it should. So, do yourself a favor and invest in the things that actually matter. Take what went terribly wrong and find the positive in it.

Focus on what you can learn from it, so you can make the situation better.

### Study Hall

1. How have you been disappointed in the past?
2. How has being disappointed affected you?
3. How have you disappointed others?
4. Was there a time when you *had* "expectations," but *should have* had an "appreciation?"
5. What are some ways you can "bounce back" from disappointment and be more "appreciative?

# *Damage*

Damage /ˈdamij/ (Verb) - To inflict physical harm on someone or something, to impair its value, usefulness, and/or function.

**LESSON** – "You are not damaged beyond repair. You are worth fixing."

*W*hen an apartment complex catches fire, the whole building doesn't usually burn down. Rather, the only part that is *fully damaged* is where the fire originally started. Although the adjoining apartments may suffer *some* damage as well, the primary focus of the damage is where the fire began.

But, even though only a couple of apartments are either partially or fully damaged, the whole building *still* must be evacuated. When this happens, no one is allowed back into the building until the apartments have been repaired.

In the beginning, firefighters and the apartment manager aren't sure how badly damaged the building is or if the structure can *still* support the weight of its residents. If residents enter the premises and the building is not safe and sound, they could be injured or killed. In addition, it could also cause further damage to the building itself.

So, after the firefighters have completed their job, officials (i.e. electric & gas company, the insurance company, construal engineers, builders, etc.) assess the damage and determine the next steps. While officials are assessing the damage, they discover two important things: (1) The entire building didn't burn down. Therefore, some parts of it can be salvaged. Thankfully, those parts are still in good condition. And, (2) some parts of the building *may* be beyond repair, and thus, need to be removed for safety reasons and rebuilt.

The good news is most of the damaged (not

destroyed) parts can be fixed to look as if nothing ever happened.

Well, guess what? That same concept can be applied to people. No one is so damaged they are beyond repair. For example, not having my biological father in my life damaged me. I was also damaged by my ex-husband and our marriage, *and* by some of the decisions, I made along the way.

Furthermore, I have been damaged by my family's words and actions. I have even been damaged without me even knowing it!

When I was in my early 20s, I was raped, even though I didn't realize it was rape at the time. Now, that I am in a more peaceful place in my life, I can openly and honestly say, "I was raped when I was in my 20s."

I didn't realize I had been raped until a documentary on "rape" came on the television, and it all came flooding back to me. It was at that moment that I felt prepared to process what really happened to me.

*I was raped.*

It was at that moment that I realized the damage I experienced because of the rape. At first, I thought it was my fault because I was drunk at the time... BUT, in truth, I remember every detail of the violation.

I remember my rapist saying, "You will *never* be anything. You'll fail at everything you do even in your old age." He also taunted me with, "No one will ever want you again, because you are damaged goods now."

I drank before the rape, but after it, I started drinking more to "escape" my feelings of shame and self-doubt.

I was also damaged when I became pregnant for the first time. I had my first child right after my 17th birthday. What followed was an abortion and miscarriage.

I had a hard time healing after having a child at such a young age, an abortion, and then a miscarriage. Why? Well, because every time I went to the doctor for a checkup, he or she would ask me about those painful times in my life.

~   *How many pregnancies have you had?*

~   *How many living children do you have?*

~   *How many miscarriages have you had?*

I was damaged once again when I lost my job *and* my first house. Truth-be-told, the damage I experienced caused me to damage other people. How? Well, I once stole over $200 worth of items from a grocery store. In other words, I did $200 worth of damage to someone else.

Then, I aborted my baby because I was pregnant by a separated, but *still* married man. I decided to abort the baby after I unexpectedly came face-to-face with his wife at an event. It was during this event that I first learned that the father of my unborn baby was married. I was shocked and hurt because I didn't know.

Yet, even after all of the embarrassment, I *chose* to stay with him. So, as you can see, I also damaged people. I manipulated people, so I could survive.

But, the person I damaged the most was my son, William. When William was 2, I left him at home alone, while I went to work. Although he was asleep when I left, this action turned into one of the scariest, most life-changing moments in my life. I left William upstairs in the bed, when I returned from work, he was not there. I thought he ran out of the door, but he was downstairs asleep in the den. I knew to lose him would have placed me in a spiral of depression.

I was horrified by what I did, but I learned, over time, that the damage I caused William was not unforgivable. Yes, the damage I caused him and others was hurtful, but there was *still* hope for me. *In other words, the damage could be repaired.* I have learned that no one is beyond repair - if he or she really wants to change and be a better person.

As I reflect on the apartment fire analogy, I can't help, but wonder why the whole building didn't burn down. Why were only a couple of apartments destroyed, instead of all of them? How were some apartments *still* salvageable and repairable, while others were not?

Now, there are some, who would say, "Just tear down the whole building and start over…" From this perspective, the building is beyond repair and nothing can be done. But, what if, it was you instead of a building? What if someone said, "YOU were damaged beyond repair?" What if those same people said that you were "unfixable" and "unlovable?"

Believe me when I say, "You can heal and be made whole after all of this." Because it's the truth. I've experienced it. Your "best parts" can help repair your "damaged parts." Your "best parts" can sustain you, while you are "being made whole again." This *allows* the undamaged parts of you to continue, while the damaged parts are healing.

Let's return to the apartment fire analogy once again. Out of an eight-unit apartment building, *only* two apartments were burned beyond repair. In other words, *only* two apartments had to be completely torn down (gutted).

After the engineers and contractors determined what they needed to repair the damage and how much it would cost, they gave the estimate to the apartment manager and the owner. Basically, the estimate said that the owner of the apartments would need to replace the support beams, because without them, the entire building would fall. It also said the owner would need to replace the walls, windows, etc.

The estimate detailed the cost of everything and how much time it will take to complete the repairs.

Guess what? An estimate can be used to help repair the damage you have experienced *and* caused others. For instance, your estimate may consist of healing, advancement, peace, and joy, instead of windows and support beams.

And, just like the estimate given to the apartment manager & owner, there is a list of "things" that need to be repaired in your life, along with the cost of repairing these "items." In other words, the things (i.e. healing, advancement, peace, and joy) you need to be repaired will cost you something. So, it's important you are prepared to do whatever it takes to make those repairs because there is truly a price to pay.

In the apartment fire analogy, the next step involves the general contractor. It is now time to write-up the contract (agreement). The contract may or may not include the costs of using some of the salvaged building. Regardless, it's a starting point. You have to start somewhere, right?

But, don't fool yourself into thinking that the damage can be quickly repaired, because it can't. Rather, it is a process. The same goes for us it takes time to heal the broken and damaged areas of our life. Even when we or others think it is beyond repair.

*So, what should we do?* Assess the damage.

Think about what needs to be repaired then tell

yourself, "I can 'bounce back' from this!"

Also, tell yourself, "I have assessed my damage, so I know what I need to do to make those repairs. Therefore, I am doing whatever it takes to repair the damage in my life." This is needed in order for you to heal productively in all areas of your life.

It's the "bounce back" that helps you grow. I like to believe that my "bounce back" has made my "comeback" even better. No, I know it has!

All of the things people said I would never do - I have done. There have always been those, who doubted me, yet, I *still* prevailed. Sometimes, I walked on broken pieces, but I *still* moved. I was hurt, but I *still* functioned. In fact, I *still* functioned through my divorce. I *still* functioned after I was raped. I *still* functioned, while I was stealing. I *still* functioned after I had an abortion. I *still* functioned after my miscarriage. And, I *still* functioned, while my family drug my name through the mud.

*Was it a great experience?* No! In fact, some

days, I was only able to function by "going through the motions." But, guess what? I was *still* moving forward, working towards repairing those damaged places in my life.

Thus, it is imperative that you be open to repairing what needs to be repaired, regardless of whatever else is happening in your life. Keep in mind that every repair will not be the same, just as every president, parent, friend, job, location or anything else is not the same. Therefore, all of your damaged areas need to be addressed at some point.

Also, keep in mind that as you are going through this repair process, you will probably notice other things that have damaged you - things that also need to be repaired. For instance, not having your father around affected you, how a situation you experienced affected you, and how raising a child or children, as a single-parent, affected you and your kids. For me, being a single-parent affected me. Therefore, when going through the repair process ask yourself:

~   What did it do for me?

~   What did it do to me?

This is important because your perception plays a significant role in the healing process. It plays a vital role in how you see yourself, others, and the world around you. It also helps you determine if and how well the damage can be repaired. Thus, this and many other factors, help you become the person you were created to be.

Another thing that played a major role in repairing my damage was having a relationship with God. Now, I'm not here to push religion or spirituality on anyone, but this is where I am right now. My spirituality is of utmost importance to me.

*I love the Lord.*

However, it's important to understand that God didn't *fix* things for me just because I said, "Fix it!" He *fixed* things for me because I was willing to put in the work for it to be *fixed*.

I realized that God always has my back, so I no longer cared if people thought I was worthy of being *fixed*. The same way, in the apartment fire analogy, people thought the building was not worth fixing. The truth is very few people know how I received salvation. It involves the scripture reference, Romans 10:9-10. I must admit that I was never really all that religious. And to be honest, I'm still not all that religious, in the traditional sense. However, I have always been a big believer in God.

Well, in 2005 when I became pregnant with a married man's baby. As I explained before, I didn't know he was married until much later. However, once I found out, I stayed with him. To be fair, he didn't know I was pregnant. We lived in two different states at the time, so it was easy for me to hide the pregnancy from him.

I was already struggling with being a single-parent and was ready to end the relationship anyway. So, I decided to abort the baby. At the time, I felt it was the right thing for me to do. And, to be honest, I *still* feel that way today. Clearly, I *still* stand by my decision.

But, after the procedure, I spiraled into depression. Understand I had battled with depression slightly for about 6 years. In the beginning, I went as far as attempting to commit suicide. When this incident happened, I thought about it, but I didn't take any action. However, my friends were able to see something was wrong. Know this; you can go into some really dark places after being damaged. During this time, the damage caused my hair to fall out, my weight was up and down, I cried all the time, and so many more things were happening. I didn't say much to other people, opting to "zone out" and cry myself to sleep instead. In all honesty, I was just "going through the motions."

Then, one Saturday, while I was working overtime, a woman named Shonda Richey came in and sat down next to me. Her spirit was magnetic because she was always smiling. Mrs. Shonda was inviting and caring towards others. I like that she gave off positive energy.

So, we sat and talked. With tears in my eyes; I told her what I had done. And, for the first time ever, I didn't feel judged, rejected, or even small. Afterward, she asked me about salvation. Thus, began the beginning of my new journey.

Keep in mind that it was not an easy journey; however, it opened me up, so I could clearly see how damaged I really was. It also opened me up so I could see what I needed to do to make it right with myself and others. So with God's help and Mrs. Shonda's encouragement, I mustered the courage to face it all head-on.

Let's return to the apartment fire analogy one last time. When you live in an apartment complex, you are usually required to purchase rental insurance for your apartment, in case of a fire or natural disaster. This insurance covers any damage to the contents of your home while giving you an opportunity to find a new temporary place to live.

The owner (of the building) purchases insurance that will cover the structure of the building only.

Yes, you may be required to start over, but at least you have *something* to start over with. That is the type of relationship I have with God - and still do.

So, after I aborted the married man's baby, I decided to tell him the truth. As you can probably guess, it did not go over too well with him. I felt terrible, so I asked for his forgiveness, even though doing so was really hard. It was worth it. At the time he didn't forgive me. Eventually, years later, we had a conversation and he did.

It was God's assurance (insurance) that gave me my *freedom*. I refused to *allow* anyone to hold what I did over my head because I was *free* now.

I want you to be *free* too. *Free* to own what happened to you. *Free* to deal with the consequences of your own actions. And lastly, *free* to move on with your life.

Don't let anyone tell you differently.

For me, it was this assurance (insurance) that ultimately *freed* me. That's why I am not ashamed to talk about all of this now. I am not afraid to talk about how God's assurance *freed* me. Well, it was the *only* thing that connected me back to my Creator. It is God's love that protects and guides me. It is God's love that I am so grateful for.

### Homework

*Assess*

I believe that we *must* take a daily assessment of our lives. We *must* know where we are and what we need to work on. In addition, we *must* assess the damage we've experienced throughout our lives. *So, ask yourself the following questions:*

- ~ What damage did you incur?
- ~ Was the damage devastating to your life?
- ~ How did it knock you off-track?
- ~ How did it affect you? Positively or negatively?
- ~ What was your initial reaction?

~ How did your reaction affect others?

***The clearer and more detailed you are, the more you'll know how to proceed. So, purchase a journal and write down your thoughts and feelings about the damaged you've experienced and caused. Then, try to answer as many of the above questions, as possible. When you are clear on the details, you can move forward with clarity.

### *Adjust*

Once you have a clear understanding of the damage that has been caused, there is an adjustment period. During this time, you will need to make the necessary changes to be fully repaired. It's also important to understand that these adjustments may be internal, external, or a combination of both. The key to making this work is being *willing* to make the necessary changes. Maybe, you can make some quick changes on some things, but not others. That is normal. Remember, repairing the damage takes time. It is a gradual process, so you *must* be committed to making those changes, as they arise.

Why is this important? Well, if you are willing to do your part, you will reap the benefits. You'll be able to *see* and *feel* the changes taking place.

### Study Hall

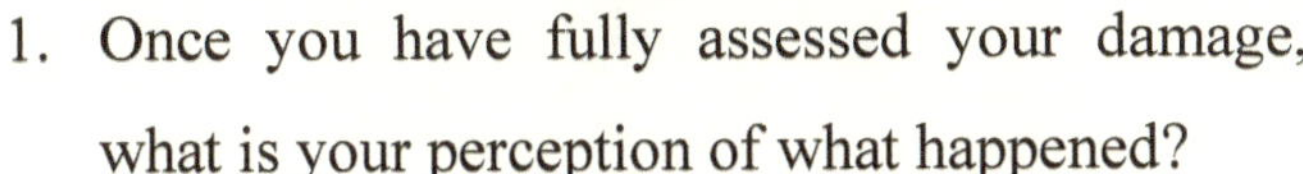

1. Once you have fully assessed your damage, what is your perception of what happened?

2. How do you feel about what happened to you? More specifically, what feelings have arisen after thinking about the damage that you have incurred and the damage you have caused others?

3. Lastly, what have you learned from this assessment? And, what can you change to repair the damage?

# Discouragement

Discouragement / ˌdisˈkərijmənt/ (Noun) - A loss of confidence or enthusiasm. An attempt to prevent something by showing disapproval or creating difficulties; a deterrent.

**LESSON** – "Listen to the voice (Holy Spirit) from within. God is always right."

Most of the time, your biggest "discourager" is yourself. And, truthfully, I have played a pivotal role in my own discouragement. The next biggest "discouragers" are the people closest to us, primarily because we value their opinions.

Think about it - if some jerk you don't know said, "You'll never be anything! You're worthless!" You'd probably brush it off and keep moving. He or she doesn't know you and you don't know him or her, so who cares what he or she thinks or says.

However, if your mother says the same thing to you, it's hurtful and maybe even devastating, because you value her opinion and want her to be proud of you.

Keep this in mind, as you read this particular chapter of the book.

When I first started my business, I wanted *everyone* to be a part of it. I was fortunate that a lot of people, who had encouraged me, had skills I really didn't have. As a result, I decided to reach out to them to see if they'd like to partner with me on projects.

Well, one day, as I was working on a getaway style project, I contacted someone close to me to tell her about the project and ask her to partner. I was so excited. I told her *every* detail… I told her what her role would be, and how great it would be to have her on the project. I also explained what her job tasks would require.

I paced back-and-forth throughout my house, as

I shared my dream with her. My heart was racing, as my smile stretched from ear-to-ear. Honestly, I was so excited; I could have run out the door and presented my vision for the business to potential investors right then.

I thought to myself, "Oh my gosh! I'm going to do A, B, and C, and it is going to be so amazing!" I did not realize, at the time, that I had just given my first business presentation.

*Let's be clear, none of this was ever about me.*

Once, I gave my pitch to other talented people I had my eye on, they were ok with the task. They were sold on the idea or had a vision of what was happening. But, although they accepted the positions, I always ended up doing most of the work. I didn't mind, because all I wanted them to do was "show up" and do their jobs. And, over time I became good at "selling" my dream to others.

Unfortunately, those I wanted to partner with would always find ways to see the vision in the most negative light. They also had a habit of saying the most hurtful things to me and about the project and the situation.

For instance, they would say things like, "Are you sure this is what you really want to do? Are you sure this is the Lord's plan for your life? Are you sure you can do this and be successful at it? Do you even know how much all of this will cost?"

I remember thinking to myself, "I am trying to put money in our pockets! I am trying to include you in my business without requiring *anything* in return! *How dare you try to kill my dreams?*"

After being on the phone for 10 or 15 minutes with a negative person, I would get fed up and tell him or her I needed to go. Because of the negativity, I usually ended up walking away from the conversation, doubting myself, my skills, and my abilities.

I'd think to myself, "Maybe, I shouldn't try to do it." I then would ask God if I should try to do it. I'd say, "Lord, should I give up on my dream? Or, is this what you have called me to do? Are you sure?"

This was when my *discouragement* turned into *doubt*. It not only made me second-guess myself but also what I knew the Lord had called me to do.

The truth is discouraging people can really knock you down and make you doubt yourself. This is a different type of *discouragement*. It is not like when you discourage yourself. Honestly, the "Negative Nellies" make you feel like you have to continually prove yourself to them. And, when you try to do just that, they *still* find something to pick at.

Let's just say, there is no pleasing them.

In their minds, you will *never* be good enough and you will *never* know enough. How dare you know more than them in *any* area?

It's these negative people, who try to talk you out of pursuing your dreams and desires. They steal your courage, confidence, and hope. They take away the very things that excite you.

So, after questioning myself and my abilities,

based on what others said or did, I realized I was the one, who was killing my joy, peace, love, and motivation to do the very things I enjoyed. The more it happened, the more I continued to understand that I just couldn't work with these people nor could I share with them (prematurely) what I was working on.

The truth is we share things with the people closest to us, especially when we are excited. We want them to share in our happiness, optimism, and joy. Most importantly, we value their opinions. In other words, we place a high value on what they say. But, honestly, what they say should *never* have that much influence over us.

In fact, there have been times when I've had to limit my conversations with others or only discuss certain subjects with them because of their energy. This includes family members, friends, and anyone else; I felt had an energy that didn't line-up with mine.

In addition, there have been places I wouldn't go because I felt it would dampen my own energy.

It was during these times that I realized I had to change, or I would *not* accomplish *anything.*

To put it all in perspective, the very people, who always had something negative to say to me or about me were the same ones, who were projecting their own insecurities, doubts, inabilities to go out and try something new, and their failure to step-out on faith, or whatever you want to call it, on me.

Frankly, I don't believe these fears had anything to do with me, as a person. Did they really want me to fail? Probably not. In fact, I believe they actually wanted me to *win.*

Their negativity stemmed from the fact that they couldn't do what I was trying to do, live out their purpose. They did not understand my vision or how to make it all work because their faith was not there.

After a discouraging phone call, the person I always reached out to was my husband. Why him? Well, because he taught me that the best way to deal with negative people is to "disengage." Just don't say anything.

According to my husband, the best thing to do in these situations is to do what you originally planned to do. He explained that they just weren't ready to be a part of the team and that was ok.

A common saying is "move in silence," but I don't believe God created us to be that way. I believe that you have to be mindful of who you share things with and who you partner with. I also believe that when God gives you a vision – it's yours, not anyone else's. But, because it's your vision (and only your vision), some people may not understand it or join you on your journey and that is ok.

And, then there are those, who hear you, but refuse to go with you for some reason. Lastly, some will cheer you on just because they are supportive. These are the people that support you from the sidelines, watching as you make your dreams come true.

But, for some others, it takes actually *seeing* you make it before they understand God's plan, vision, and mission for your life.

However, I have learned a few things about sharing your vision with people, especially those, who *say* they support you, but their actions say the exact opposite. I have learned that it is ok to be quiet during these times. I have also learned to only share certain things with certain people – the ones, who really understand where I was and where I want to go.

For example, I only share business-related plans with my "sista-friends," because they encourage me, give me the best advice, and are honest with me.

My "sista-friends" have their own businesses. The best thing about this group of women is that when we are together, we don't care who is around. We just talk. We bounce ideas off of each other, causing our conversations to go to another level. And just like that, we become super excited for each other.

I should record our gab sessions one day

because honestly, they are pretty hilarious. We laugh and brainstorm so much we often forget what we were initially talking about.

There are also people, who I don't feel comfortable telling *anything* to, especially when it comes to my business goals and dreams. Why not? Well, because when I share these things with them, they always have something negative to say.

*I don't want to hear that.*

So, for that reason, I *choose* not to share this information with them. I make a deliberate *choice* to *only* talk about certain things with them. So, if they ask about my business, I say, "Everything's going great!"

I will never tell them about my accomplishments because I know they will say something negative. I also will never tell them about my million-dollar clients because I know they will not understand. I'm not trying to be offensive, but it's the truth.

I've learned I can't talk to *some* people about

my vision, because they simply won't get it. More specifically, they won't understand my progress and growth. So, I *only* share things with them once I have achieved my goals.

I have learned to be quiet with them. I'm not saying you shouldn't share your vision with others, rather, use the spirit of discernment to know who to talk to and who not to.

Also, don't feel like you have to explain *everything* to *everyone*. I don't have to justify anything and neither do you. If the Lord tells you to go into a burning building and someone asks you, "Why do you want to go into a burning building? Why are you doing that?" Don't feel like you have to justify your actions to him or her, if that is truly what the Lord told you to do.

The truth is more often than not, you have to fight through discouragement, especially when things don't go the way you'd hoped. Honestly, every time I have attempted to do something, it has gone wrong. Did that kill the entire project? No.

Did it kill me? No. Did it hurt? Absolutely.

While writing this book, I battled a situation that went terribly wrong. It hurt because it involved people I cared about.

These individuals accused me of creating debt in someone else's name. They also accused me of trying to sabotage them. More specifically, I was accused of stealing from a client when in actuality they stole from me.

The thing is my job, at the time, involved using my business's name to sign most of my client contracts. When my client amassed a balance, I paid it off for them. Yes, it was stupid, but it was more of a relationship-building thing.

Well, I eventually grew tired of paying off my clients' debts, that's when I was accused of doing terrible things. This particular client felt like I was attempting to ruin their reputation because I stopped paying off their debt. Then, it all went downhill from there.

This situation made me reconsider having a

business or even wanting to plan events anymore. After that, I decided to make some changes. I simply couldn't stay in a place of discouragement.

Now, one of the things I often tell my friends and my son is that it is far easier for a train to slow down and start back up, than for it to completely stop and then re-start all over again.

In other words, don't *allow* discouragement or roadblocks to derail you from what you want to do. If you give "discouragers" that much power over you, you will never accomplish anything. Yet, if you push forward, you'll just have taken it as a lesson learned.

Also, keep in mind that when people discourage you, it's a projection of their own fears, anxieties, and worries. Don't *allow* these individuals to make you doubt yourself, because at some point, the doubt will turn into fear.

*Fear is real and it will prevent you from moving forward.*

We all have fears. I become afraid every time I

attempt to do something new and unfamiliar. In fact, every time I make a decision, my heart starts beating really quickly, and I begin to think to myself, "Is this right? Should I do this? Should I talk about this with anyone?"

But, I press on anyway, fighting through my fears. That's why I'm not surprised that my best work comes when I'm afraid. But the truth is I don't always know if things are going to work out in my favor. Yet, I continue, doing what I have been called to do, believing it will.

You see, not only do people cause you to doubt yourself; they can also trigger self-discouragement. In fact, there have been days when I've become so discouraged or doubtful that I considered seeking employment.

However, the closest I've ever gotten to doing that is looking up jobs on the computer. I've never actually applied for other jobs. I don't know why. No, wait, I do know why. It's because a small part of me – a part I like to call the "Holy Spirit" speaks to me. It is this part of me that prevents me from giving up.

Because of this, I realize that working a nine-to-five job to build-up someone else's company is not what God has called me to do. It's also not what I want to do with my life.

It was my own self-discouragement that caused me to look for other job options. It was my own self-doubt that caused me to question myself and God's plan for me and my life.

Honestly, I have tried to quit my business many times, but His calling has always prompted me to stay still. It is a part of who I am. It is in my DNA. When you know what you're supposed to be doing, you get called back every time. God won't let you go to the left when you're really supposed to go to the right.

But, this is where doubt and discouragement come into play. Then, you have to say to yourself, "You know what? I'm going to keep going forward no matter what. Even if I only complete one task today, I'm still going to keep moving forward."

Bottom line - don't *allow* yourself to be derailed by doubt and discouragement.

Also, don't overly share "things" (what you are doing) with negative people, because they will only discourage you. I don't believe their ultimate goal is to "hate on you." That's not what it is. More specifically, it's not that they doubt your abilities. I believe it's something within themselves that has caused them to regret the things they *should've* done.

People question themselves. And, because they are frustrated with themselves, it is projected towards you, as discouragement and doubt. It's a tiny voice that causes them to say to you, "You shouldn't do it either."

And, guess what? It's not even really about you! It's a personal thing. Nevertheless, you must take the discouragement and doubt with a "grain of salt." These individuals are battling something internally. I have always heard that jealousy comes in several forms, but trust me, this is *not* jealously. It is self-doubt.

There have also been times when I didn't do what I should have done or didn't get what I was supposed to get, but even then I *still* tried. Do I still get discouraged? Of course. Do I still have doubts? Of course. But, when you have a circle of family and friends, who know the *real* you, and who can say to you, "Now that you are done pouting - get it together!" You *see* things differently.

It is these people, who become your support system. They are the ones, who *always* help you get back on track. They are the ones, who *always* provide you with constructive criticism. They are the ones, who *always* ask you the hard questions like, "What is your plan?" "How are you going to move forward?" "What have you decided to invest in?"

You must have a strong, positive support system if you are going to overcome doubt and discouragement.

## Homework

### *Affirm*

I place affirmations all around me. However, I have learned that affirmations don't mean anything, if you don't believe in them. So, I use these affirmations to prompt me to act. So, when I say, "I earn $13,700, per day," I try to visualize what that type of money actually looks like and what kind of day someone earning that has. I then say to myself, "What do I need to do to accomplish this goal?" I also tell myself, "I am a loving, caring, and supportive wife." But, what does that actually look like? What should it look like? And, does my husband feel that from me?

Affirmations are good reminders of what God says about us and what he has in store for us. So, use present tense and write them down. Then, surround yourself with them to remind yourself of what you need to focus on. After that, record yourself reading the affirmations, then listen to them, as you exercise and perform tasks. Use them as part of your personal development. Say them out loud to help you combat self-doubt and discouragement.

## *Assign*

This word has two forms. The first one involves "assigning" particular conversations to particular people. As I stated before, there are certain topics, I only speak to certain people about. Then, there are other topics I only speak to God about. Which is everything. And, I don't cross those lines, once I have made that decision. This prevents me from becoming discouraged. It also helps me focus on my purpose. The second part involves knowing and understanding one's "assignment." This helps me put my energy into what I have been called to do. It also helps me stick with my decisions, regardless of what anyone has to say about them. *Is it easier said than done?* Sometimes.

For instance, let's take this book - I have known the title and what I wanted to write about for at least 3 years. Yet, I procrastinated about it. Then, pre-sales began and I *still* procrastinated about it. But, God kept on me, so I pushed myself to remember why I was writing it in the first place. I discouraged myself by worrying about whether or not others were going to read or purchase my book. I also worried about what people would say about it after they read it. However, the truth is, the book was really about me walking into *freedom*. So, I knew I had to press on.

## Study Hall

1.  List affirmations you feel will help you better understand who you are and what you have been called to do.

2.  List the people you talk to on a regular basis. What are some things you have to stop talking to them about because they are discouraging?

3.  What are some things you have been procrastinating about? Why? And, now that you acknowledge this, how can you encourage yourself to complete these tasks?

# Distance

Distance /ˈdistəns/ (Noun) - An amount of space between two things or people. The condition of being far off; remoteness.

**LESSON** – "Absence not only makes the heart grow fonder; it also gives you peace."

*I* am the eldest of my mother's three children and (technically) the eldest of my father's ten children. I say "technically" because my oldest brother is deceased.

At the age of 6, I began attending summer camp, as soon as school let out. In fact, school would get out for summer break one week and I would be off to camp the next week.

I attended several camps during the summer. And, by the time I returned home from camp, at the end of July, it was time for our "family vacation." Our "family vacations" typically occurred during the first or second week of August. However, once the vacation was over, it was time to return to school.

We took vacations every year, and because of them (the vacations), I now have a deeper desire to explore what the world has to offer.

Fortunately, I got to visit most of the southeastern region of the United States, before I even turned 14. Thank you, mom, grandmother, and grandfather for introducing me to and nurturing my love for traveling. My love for traveling also planted the seed for my interest in the hospitality industry.

So, outside of being gone all summer I spent most of my time with my grandparents, William & Carrie Coachman. They also helped raise me and literally lived next door. In fact, the only thing that separated our house from theirs was the three fruit trees that my grandmother planted.

Although my mom was present, during this time, she also had my brothers to take care of. So, my grandparents mainly took care of me. And, to be honest, it was kind of weird. We were together yet separate at the same time. As a result, I felt like an only child for most of my life.

My mom was a single-parent, so when my twin brothers came along, it was almost too much for her to deal with all of us. I also had other siblings on my father's side, but he wasn't really present in their lives either - with the exception of my youngest sister.

Because I was always with my grandparents growing up, I now connect more with older people. I believe the reason I've never had separation issues is because I was mostly alone, as a child. In other words, it doesn't bother me to be by myself. I realize that's not necessarily a good thing, especially when it comes to having long-term relationships. I'm still working on opening myself up to others because it doesn't come naturally to me.

I think this is why I always felt alone, as a child. Outside of my school friends, there really weren't any other kids around my age in my family. Plus, I was the only girl in the house. Thus, I was always with older people - really older people.

I also didn't have separation anxiety because I was always gone - or the people I loved were always gone. As a result, I assumed that being alone and people leaving was just a part of life.

But, I felt different about it when my husband was deployed. I will talk about that in a later chapter.

But, even now, as an adult, if my family (husband and son) and my "sista-friends" don't hear from me for a few days when I travel, I always hear about it. I don't do it on purpose…I'm usually just in the moment - doing what I need to do. I don't think about it, because if I'm absolutely honest, I never had anyone genuinely miss me.

So, for someone (my husband, son, and "sista-friends") to have a genuine concern about me is something new for me - it is something I have had to get used to and accept because I love them.

But because of my childhood, distance doesn't really bother me. The thing is, when people really care about you, it makes a difference in your life. Honestly, I kind of like the distance, because it creates a balance for me. If I'm honest, I can only experience certain people and things for a certain amount of time and then I am done.

In my family dynamic, outside of my son and husband, I've always been ok with distance. In fact, I've always viewed this distance as "normal." For me, distance doesn't mean "I don't love you or care about you" - it simply means that "I'm over here and you are over there."

I believe there is a time to be together and a time to be a part. Distance is not a bad thing. It gives me quiet time to think and process things. It allows me to sit in my office and be ok with being alone - be ok with being just with me.

I don't have to be in the presence of people.

Although, I love talking to people and I enjoy meeting new people. In fact, even as an adult, I find myself talking to myself. I give presentations to myself, and my family catch me doing it all of the time. They think it is funny, but I am ok with being with me

On the flip side, distance is also something we do to "escape" other people and circumstances. We do this so we don't have to face them head-on. So, although you may need a minute to process something, you *still* need to handle the situation. Because these situations won't go away simply because you distance yourself.

## Homework

### *Boundaries*

Putting distance between you and other people or things, so you can evolve, as a human being, is totally necessary. The truth is there are some people, who need to live at least 2-hours away from me. Just being honest. Some can be closer because I know they aren't going to "pop up" for a visit without notice. There are also events and places I won't go to, even when I am invited because there is a lack of clear boundaries. These boundaries are important to me. It is important to make boundaries clear to others. My peace is far more important than doing what everyone else wants me to do.

### Associate

Have you heard the saying, "Birds of a feather flock together?" Well, we tend to do more explaining when it comes to who we associate with or what actions we take than on putting some distance between us and others. Think about it - if you are hanging with a particular group of people or you're in a particular location all of the time, you are considered to be associated with that group or location. Therefore, to maintain your integrity, strength, and self-worth, you must put distance between you and certain people and/or you and certain locations to retain your sense of self.

The thing is, sometimes, the people and things

you associate with don't have your best interest at heart. You stay with them because of blind loyalty or because you want their acceptance. But, the truth is, you need to create distance between you and those people and things in order to change your situation.

It is important to disassociate yourself from those, who aren't good for you and those, who don't fit with the vision you have for your life. Keep in mind that not everyone will go with you to the next level, the next place, the next promotion, or even the next neighborhood.

In some cases, you can maintain your relationship, but in others, you cannot. So, you will have to make the appropriate adjustments.

### Study Hall

1.  What are some people, places or things you need to distance yourself from?

2.  In what areas do you need to set boundaries?

3.  What boundaries have you put in place?

# Deployment

Deployment /dəˈploimənt/ (Noun) - The movement of troops or equipment to a place or position for military action.

**LESSON** – "They were right; it will never be the same."

M ilitary spouses have a special place in my heart because I was one - I am one. I guess even after your spouse retires, you are *still* considered a military spouse. My husband, Marcus LaCroix, served the United States for well over 10 years in the *United States Marine Corps*. He was truly committed to his country, and, honestly, I couldn't be prouder of him. I truly honor him.

Throughout his tenor in the military, we lived

together for 2-years, that's all. He was gone a lot of the time. So, I thought I was prepared when he told me that he was being sent to the Middle East for a year. My husband being away was just another form of distance – one I thought I could handle. I was a single mom when I met him; so, I thought I'd be ok with him leaving me and William by ourselves. I was wrong.

Preparing for my husband to leave was both hard and long. Between the trainings, meetings, and legal paperwork, I felt like I was leaving for the Middle East too.

And, because the process is so taxing, I send my love and respect to spouses, who have been through this process multiple times.

In the process of preparing for my husband's tour in the Middle East, I asked him, "Are you coming back?" It's hard to talk about what could happen when a loved one is deployed, but it's important.

Some people don't come home and some come

home with missing or damaged body parts. I just wanted him to be honest with me. But, if you are married to a member of the *United States Marine Corps* (or any military branch for that matter), your spouse may never want to talk about what could happen or has happened to them in the past. They may not want to talk about what they saw either. So, save yourself the headache, and don't ask him or her. This advice may be hard to swallow, but I'm trying to help you.

My husband told me he was either coming home or not. There was no in-between. I, like you, wanted to know what that meant. Well, that meant that if my husband lost a limb, an eye, or anything else, he wouldn't return home. He would prefer to die in combat. In other words, he would not *allow* me to take care of him afterward.

As much as I wanted to fight him on this, it was his decision, so I had to accept it.

A few things happened to me from the time he left to the time he returned. Being alone was cool for the most part. I think that the best part was that I had the bed to myself. Aghhh…. yes, I slept in the middle. And, I could watch what I wanted on TV and William and I ate out most of the time.

No more *Discovery* channel, *History* channel, and *Law & Order* (I like the show, but he overdoes it). It was all about the *Travel* channel now. Nevertheless, when he left, I couldn't sleep because I had not heard from him. My body was saying *sleep*, but my eyes were telling me to *stay awake*. So, for almost three days straight, I ran on 2-hours of sleep, a day.

Then, he finally called me from Germany, and we spoke all of 5-minutes. Ironically, I told him I had to go because I was sleepy. I was relieved after that. You may think that was mean of me to get off the phone so quickly, but my husband understood.

Again, he was gone all the time, so I thought I could handle the time apart. Remember, I don't have separation issues.

Well, I was totally wrong, but not for the

reason you think. When he went on deployment, I was cool. I knew how to deal with the car and pump my own gas. I also knew how to pay bills - that was not new to me. I also knew how to take care of our house, myself, and our son because I was already doing those things. Therefore, he did not have to worry about me holding down "The LaCroix House," while he was away.

But, his deployment really messed me up mentally. I didn't have any emotional support. As I mentioned before, when I finally got his phone call and knew he was ok, sleep was all I wanted.

There were many times, we talked for hours. There was always something for us to talk about. Still, I rarely addressed any problems with him because I felt he needed to focus on his job and safety. Plus, there wasn't anything I couldn't handle on my own. Sometimes, I rattled on so long I would have to stop and ask him, "Am I talking too much?"

He would always say, "No," of course, probably because he didn't know when we would get to talk again.

While he was gone, I had my first event of the year. Until this point (he had been away 6-months on training and had not officially left the country), I had not shed one tear, but during the event, I let it all go. I cried like a baby. I thought about having to rearrange my entire work schedule and being the only parent in the home again. It broke me to my core.

When we got married, we agreed

that William would always have at least one parent present, and this was one of those times. God had always *allowed* us to stay true to this agreement.

When I was traveling, my husband would be present with our son and vice versa. We never had anything going on simultaneously that caused both of us to be gone at the same time. So, when my husband was on deployment, I only took events in the summertime or on the weekends.

Now, back to this event – One day, William

and I were packing the car, getting ready to get on the road. I don't think William had his permit or was taking Driver's Ed at the time. I remember thinking to myself, "I'm really doing this without my husband."

Keep in mind that I left the night before the event. But, before I left I went into my bedroom to make sure I had everything. Then, it happened. I dropped to the floor and began sobbing. I realized that my husband would not be there.

There would be no one to drive me around, help me set-up for the event, or accompany while I ran errands. I know I sound spoiled or petty, but this is a family business – my dream.

I was used to him driving me around, while I worked on my laptop. Marcus would also handle certain things, so I could focus on my presentation. Furthermore, my husband and son would pack the car for me.

My husband isn't only my spouse; he is also my best friend and my business partner. There are things I say to him that others, outside of God, would think is crazy. Nothing else has broken me, but that did. The amazing thing is, while I was on the floor crying, he called. Yeah, it made it worse, but it also helped.

But, he didn't even comfort me. No, he said something like, "Get it together! We have a business to run. You can cry later." I wasn't offended because that is what I needed to hear to refocus.

Guess what? I made it through. William and I did 10 events that year. And, I learned so much business-wise that it was worth it.

The final thing I want to talk about is when our servicemen and women come home. I remember being in what they call the "Welcome Home Brief." This occurs when a service member is about to come home from deployment, and they warn you that your loved one may not be the same person that left you. I remember hearing that over and over again.

I refused to believe it, though, opting to "cast it down" instead. But, my husband really was different after he returned. And, because he wasn't the same person, we had to adjust, adjust again, and then adjust again. There were things we couldn't say or do. There were also certain places we couldn't go because it could trigger something inside of him.

But, because we went through it all, as a family, it wasn't hard to make those changes. My husband *still* has not told me what happened to him over there. In the beginning, it was hurtful because he wouldn't talk to me about it, but now, I understand more clearly why it is so hard for him to share that part of his life with me.

After he returned from the Middle East, my husband would sit in a room and refuse to do anything. Sometimes, William and I felt like we were walking on eggshells. I wasn't offended; I just wanted to understand why.

I realized that things happened to him, so he

had to adjust to a place that is totally different from the one he had just left. This is why I suggest you don't ask your loved one about his or her combat experiences. If he or she wants you to know, he or she will tell you.

Counseling helped our family a lot. We received counseling in 2013-2014 and in 2018. I'd be lying if I said I'm not *still* dealing with the residual effects of my husband's military experiences because I am. I'm not sure it will ever go completely away. I've had to build-up my life with the pieces that were left.

I have been around military people all of my life. I am a military child and my spouse is a *Marine*, so my perspective is different. You have to be compassionate to be the spouse of a service member. The things your spouse has seen and experienced is mind-blowing. With that understanding, my prayer is that life is better and my mind is more open to other perspectives of life.

## Homework

*Adjust*

My husband's military career taught me an important lesson on "adjustment." More specifically, I learned what it means to be married, yet single. Deployment says you are married, yet you are forced to do tasks, as a single person. The marriage part of me has always been loyal and committed. I made a covenant agreement; after all, so I have never cheated or talked to other men. That's where my marriage - my loyalty, commitment to my marriage, and commitment to the process come into play. The single part involves my independence. I had to do everything on my own, while my husband was away. I couldn't just pick up the phone and call him, because I didn't know where he was or how to reach him. But, I was blessed because I had an older child. I didn't have any young children to worry about. So "hats off" to spouses, who have to care for young children alone, while their spouses are deployed because it is a challenge.

You have to be resilient and you have to know how to make quick "adjustments." There is often no time to process it all because things are happening so quickly. As I mentioned before, there was a huge "adjustment," after my husband came home. We basically had to re-learn each other, because we were so different now. It was almost like we were dating all over again. We got to create new memories and experience new things together.

I will say this; prayer got me through many of these "adjustments." Because I didn't know the man that came home, I didn't know what he needed. It was a day-by-day process for me to understand that what he had experienced changed his life forever – and mine too.

## (Don't) Break Down

Don't forget about yourself. You have hopes, dreams, aspirations, and ambitions that didn't change just because you got married. Don't use the military or the fact that you have to move all the time, as justification, as to why you can't be you and do what you want to do. You just have to be a little more creative than everyone else. Don't live in the shadows of your spouse's career.

*Be independent.* In other words, remember that you are strong all by yourself. Having a spouse just makes you all that much stronger. *Keep yourself up.* It may sound superficial, but make sure your hair is styled and you are dressed every day. If you enjoy getting your nails done - do it! When you feel good about yourself you are more willing to be active in your own life. In other words, your self-esteem and self-confidence skyrockets and you're able to produce great and mighty things. So, don't let the fact that you have children or a spouse justify letting yourself go. One of the main reasons I added this chapter is because I watched people lose themselves after marrying a military person. They lost their abilities to take care of themselves. So, love yourself enough to *choose* yourself and achieve your goals.

### Ascertain

You are not defined by your spouse or your spouse's career. The funny thing is, there are people, who knew me before I knew them. Our last name is not common, but my husband had a habit of telling others our "business." In a positive way. So, there were wives, who were upset, because their husbands would come home and say LaCroix's wife is doing this or that. My husband is a proud man and I can't fault him for that. But, I would have to tell these wives to do what they wanted to do. I said to them, "Don't let the military stop you." Be creative, find a way, and don't make excuses. Figure it out.

I am not defined by what my husband does. I didn't marry a *Marine*, I married Marcus LaCroix, who happens to work (and is now retired) for the *United States Marine Corps*. I knew what I was signing up for when I married him. I knew he was *not* going to be home much. I knew they could call him in the middle of the night, or when we were on vacation. Yes, I missed him when he was away, however; I had my own goals and dreams and I still do. So, I had something to occupy my time. Don't get frustrated with what someone else is doing. Get up, get out, and do something!

Also, don't live in the shadows of your spouse's and your children's goals, rather, go out and make a difference. In other words, make things happen for you.

### Study Hall

1.  Have you adjusted to the changes in your life?
2.  Have you become so many things to so many people that you've lost yourself?
3.  List the parts of yourself that have been lost and detail how you plan to get them back.

# Daddy

Daddy/ˈdadē/ (Noun) - One's father. The oldest, best, or biggest example of something.

**LESSON** – "There is more to being a dad than having children. You don't have to father children to teach them. Also, you are not the only one with 'daddy issues.' Deal with them, so you can be *free*."

*I* was going to call this chapter, "Daddy, Baby Daddy, and Daddy." Yet, I think you'll get the gist of what I am trying to say.

About 10 years ago, I realized I had "daddy issues." You see, when I was born, my dad was in the military and my mother worked on the military base. I don't really know the entire story of how they got together. Even now, as an adult, I am *still* trying to piece this information together. So, I'll start here.

*Tell your children the truth.*

Regardless of how it may hurt you and them – *tell them the truth*. But, make sure they are mature enough to handle the truth.

Growing up, my grandfather, William James Coachman Sr., was the male parental figure in my life. In my mind, he was my dad, so I rarely called him "grandfather." Understand that me, of all my cousins (I am number 4 in the line) was the only one who stayed with him from birth until his death.

My cousins may think they are, but I was his "favorite". No, one can tell me differently. He raised me as if I was his daughter – not granddaughter.

He would cut out newspaper clippings with my accomplishments and show them off. I am the only grandchild that knows all of my great aunts and uncles by name and spent time with all of them. As a matter of fact, people often say how my grandfather used to take this little girl places with him all the time. They don't realize that the little girl was me.

I would also go with him to Georgetown, South Carolina, a town next door to us. That was our "thing" after school. We made several stops, so sometimes I did my homework in the car. I was tired, but he wouldn't let me sleep.

He taught me how to take care of myself and support myself. He also taught me to have a good work ethic and the importance of having good business relationships.

I learned how to do yard work from him and "handyman work," as well. Truth-be-told, I learned a lot from him and my grandmother too. My grandparents taught me how to think for myself. They taught me that there is a time and place for everything, but they *still* allowed me to express myself - even when I wasn't supposed to.

So, I questioned everything and *still* do today. In fact, if you ask my husband he will tell you that I debate all the time. But, from my perspective, I just want to understand things. I am a talker, but that came from my grandfather teaching me how to have open, honest, and direct conversations with people.

He also taught me about family and community. Now, I get why they prayed so hard for me. It was because I was never satisfied with the things people told me.

*Thinking for yourself is important.*

So, learn to do it because it will change your life.

One thing my grandmother taught me was the importance of honoring my grandfather's role in my life and in our family. In other words, she taught me to honor his role as her husband and as my dad. For instance, we didn't eat until he sat down at the table.

To be honest, I used to be hungry a lot but did not dare go into the kitchen or touch that pot of food *until* my grandfather arrived. So, it taught me to give honor where honor is due.

The foundation of what I know came from my grandfather. He set the tone for a lot of things in my life. And, even though I may have gone off the path of what he taught me, or said or done things I shouldn't have said or done, or been with people I shouldn't have been with…I never lost the foundation he built for me.

That is why I have nothing, but respect and love for him. He and my grandmother implanted God into me by living a godly life.

My biological father is a different story altogether. I met him for the first time when I was about 14. I may have met him before then, but that is what I could remember. However, he was not present in my life until I became an adult. Do I think his decision to be absent from my life had something to do with me? No. Do I think his absence had something to do with my parent's relationship or lack thereof? Absolutely.

One of the things I remember vividly is that my dad did not even call me on a couple of my birthdays. My mom called him to either remind him of my upcoming birthday or to argue with him and hang up the phone- I'm not sure which one. But, as soon as she did that, he would call back and tell me "Happy Birthday." This happened for years.

She also sent me birthday cards, signing his name, as if they came from him. I never told her I knew they were from her. My brothers and I would make long lists of the things we wanted for Christmas. I knew my mom could not afford to buy us those gifts, but I thought "Santa" could. But, even then, I often wondered how "Santa" would be able to get all of the things we wanted.

So, one Christmas, while I was supposed to be asleep, I caught her unpacking boxes. That's when I realized the "gifts" were coming from my dad. #Fraud. That was the last time I believed in "Santa Claus." But, here is the thing; my dad is who he is. I'm not going to defame him, but I am going to be honest. He was not around when I was growing up, and there is no excuse for that.

Do I understand? Yes, but that will never make it right. I get that he was in the military and had other children. I get that his lifestyle, at the time, was not conducive to what I needed in my life. But, I *still* needed my dad.

Then, in 2013, I found out I had another brother. He and my twin brothers are approximately 30-days apart in age. The truth is my dad couldn't be a father to me or any of my siblings. Honestly, at that time in his life, he just couldn't do it. It took me a long time to understand that the best thing he could have done for me, at the time, was allow my grandparents to raise me.

But, what *still* hurts is knowing he took care of other women's children - children that were not even his. But, he couldn't take care of his biological children… He paid child support, but that was it. We needed more from him.

When my siblings and I were young, our parents could do no wrong. In our minds, they knew everything. They were superheroes to us. But, as we grew older, we realized that our parents aren't perfect. That's when I began to judge them. I judged my mom for favoring my brothers over me. She loved and cared for them in a way she didn't do for me.

I judged my dad for abandoning me. I judged him for favoring someone else's children over me and my siblings. Even though, he loved my younger sister and was always present in her life – just not ours.

Truth-be-told, she is the only one of us who didn't get "left behind." But, that didn't help my anger or rage. People would say to me, "Look at what you have! You should count your blessings!"

The thing is there is a part of every little girl that feels *abandoned* when you are unwanted and unloved by a parent. It crosses your mind at some point. And, the length of time that you stay in this mental space is determined by your motivation to heal and move forward with your life.

This process took almost 10-years for me to complete. From the age of 21 to the age of 29, I was on a journey of healing. It was a tough road, but I was determined to be *free*.

Also, during that time, I was going through a bad marriage and not talking to any of my family members except for my dad's sister. It wasn't because I didn't want the support; rather, it was because I had unresolved issues with them. At that time, it had been 2-years since my grandmother passed.

By this time, the two people (my grandparents) that had always had my back were in Heaven. But during the process of healing, I was able to forgive my parents for how they treated me when I was a child. During this journey, I also re-connected with God. I had a *real* connection with Him for the first time, and because of this connection, my perspective changed.

I no longer saw my dad, as just a man, who hurt me, but rather as a man, who had been hurt himself. The burdens he carried was too heavy for him to bear. Thus, he did not have the proper mental, physical, or emotional state to be the dad I needed him to be.

Many of us need to heal from our pasts. That is why I hate it when people nonchalantly say, "Just let it go!" I say to you, "Don't let it go! You need to heal from it first." Whatever "it" is.

Acknowledge, address, and alleviate what hurt you, so you can be *free* of it. If you don't heal from it, the thing(s) you thought you "let go" will continue to show up in other areas of your life, and you will continuously wonder why. Furthermore, you will continue to judge people based on your hurt without truly understanding the root of that hurt.

So, even though I understood what my dad's mental, emotional and physical capacity was at the time, it *still* didn't make what he did *right*. Period.

My dad, to this day, has not apologized for the damage he caused me and my brothers. At first, I would scream at him when I called him. It was the little girl in me, who felt abandoned and hurt, crying out to be heard with clarity and understanding.

My dad would simply respond with, "What do you want from me?" All I wanted was an apology. But, guess what? That never happened. That is why today, I have a different perspective on the situation. I *decided* to forgive him. At this point, an apology doesn't even matter. Why not? Well, mainly because I am no longer tied to that experience.

So, even though, I understood his mind-frame at the time, I refuse to be tied to that experience. I said what I needed to say to be *free* of it. I am now *free* to move on with my life. I no longer need his approval, love, and acceptance. Seeking those things forces us to understand that our actions are not based on a true love of oneself, but rather, the acceptance of someone else.

Another reason his apology no longer matters is because when you apologize you are basically admitting you wronged someone – and I'm pretty sure he doesn't think he wronged me or my brothers. Although he did. I believe if he felt he did anything wrong he would have apologized to us a long time ago. He didn't.

We *must* sit in our truths. It's also important to understand that our actions can affect future generations. This is why we have generational curses, diseases, wealth, poverty, religious beliefs, differences, etc. The next generation has to deal with our burdens, whether they are good or bad. It is also why fathers (and mothers too) who abandon their children are also products of abandonment. The results are the same each and every time.

Knowing that you have "daddy issues" is also important for your healing. My father-in-law was in the home with his children, and my husband still had "daddy issues" to work out. The truth is there are people, who are battling so much because they haven't figured out their true issue(s).

However, I would rather be *free* than be held hostage to "grudges." This is why I thank God for my grandfather. He stood in the gap. When he passed away, I was broken - broken because I felt that I had no one now.

During my grandfather's funeral, I was surprised to get a card from my dad. He honored my grandfather in the role he played in my life and for that, I will forever be grateful. Don't get me wrong, I love my biological dad (that's what I call him). After all, we share the last name "Bragg."

And, in my heart, I know he created me to be something great so I celebrate that. However, when I was going through the healing process, I cried. And, I called him in anger and rage. Yet, he *still* wouldn't apologize to me. I don't think he understood where I was coming from at the time.

Then, I tried to get him to apologize again, but he *still* wouldn't do it. After the second time, I decided to "take a minute." As I said before, I had a lot going on at the time. But after a while, I wrote him a letter after I married my current husband.

I was already *free* at this point, however, I felt like there was a small piece of me that was *still* dealing with an unresolved issue. So, I wrote him a letter - a letter that did not contain any negativity. It only contained love. I told him that I forgave him and loved him and that there was nothing he could do to change this.

I sent him pictures of my family and told him that it did not matter what he said or did, at the end of the day, I *still* loved him. I told him I loved him with God's love *and* with a daughter's love.

I'll never forget it. I mailed the letter and experienced peace over the situation and never looked back. I felt good and you want to know what happened after that? We started talking. We may not talk every day, but we *still* talk. We're in a much better place now.

We've actually been in a great place for years. He loves my husband. He even asks about him. He also came to see me graduate with a master's degree. He's my dad. So, I no longer dwell on what happened in the past. I don't hold it against him. After I healed, I was able to let it go. But, I also no longer have certain "expectations" of him. I just want him to be himself… So, now I just go with the flow.

The truth is we know when something is missing, so we try to self-medicate with things that are not good for us. It can be anything from men to drugs to shopping.

Know this - God gives us what we need. It may not come in the way we "expect" it or hoped it would, but that's ok. I realized this later on. So, even though, God sent my grandfather to fill a void in my life, I *still* went off path.

Although, this chapter is about fathers, it also includes mothers. Elizabeth Wilson is NOT my biological mother. I love her so much, but I had to ask God to forgive me when it came to her. Though, He placed her in my life when I needed someone the most. I was chasing this mirage of what a mother *should be*. Because my biological mother was unable to be what I needed and in some cases, still unable to be what I need her to be.

But, I now realize that Elizabeth gives me what

I need from a mom at this stage in my life. She has had my back, even when she didn't agree with me and for that, I am grateful. It's important to give honor, where honor is due. It is also important to appreciate what you have and I appreciate her so much.

Let's talk about my "baby daddy issues." I will refer to him as "The Man That Shall Not Be Named (TMTSNBN)", for the remainder of this chapter. I was 16 when I got pregnant with William. My son, even when he was younger, could have come across TMTSNBN and not even known he was his father. I never talked to William about him, unless he asked me because I had nothing good to say about him.

When you don't have anything good to say about someone or something, you say nothing, right? I didn't want William to grow up in a single-parent home, but unfortunately, that is exactly what happened...for a little while anyway. I thought me and TMTSNBN would at least be able to co-parent together, but that didn't happen.

What hurts the most was seeing TMTSNBN with his new girlfriend and her children. These were the times, in which I had to *hold my mule*. In other words, I had to be quiet. For instance, William and I went to visit him one day, and he took William the *Family Dollar* to get clothes. Granted, I love a great thrift store, but "TMTSNBN" had on brand new *Jordans*. Yet, he wanted to purchase Family Dollar clothes and shoes for our son.

While we were there, he complained about how expensive school clothes and school supplies were. I thought to myself, "William is your only child, and you haven't even bought him a pencil."

On another occasion, "TMTSNBN" sent a photo of himself to William. Maybe, William wanted to know what his father looked like. That was not the problem. The problem was the photo he sent. The photo had him and a little boy in it. The little boy was sitting on his lap. The caption stated that it was his son and they'd just finished doing something together.

I know some may say that is not a problem, but it stirred something up in William. TMTSNBN had never been around or much of a dad to him, so it hurt William to see TMTSNBN with another little boy "doing things." It was this anger the caused William to "act out" and be suspended from school. I am grateful to the Principal because she didn't expel him, although she could have. Honestly, I had an out-of-body experience on both occasions, yet I *still* maintained my composure.

I had come to terms with the fact that my choices were the reason I was in this position. They were also the reason why my son had begun to "act out." But, I was *still* angry. It was the type of anger and rage that would make a lioness maul other animals over her cub.

It doesn't matter how old our children get, we *still* experience rage when we feel they are being hurt or treated unfairly. So even though, I have never really spoken openly about TMTSNBN - when I think about what my son experienced because of TMTSNBN, I get angry all over again.

Nevertheless, TMTSNBN would call sparingly and I would let William talk to him. Afterward, William would tell me about the conversation and my response would be vague. I wasn't about to show my rage to William, but it *still* hurt. It hurt to see my son in pain because of something TMTSNBN did or did not do for him.

In 2004 and 2005, I worked for an insurance company. During this time, I requested an increase in child support payments. At the time, I was *supposed* to get about $28.07, but he wasn't even paying that consistently. This arrangement had been in place since 1999. In 2004, William was about seven years old.

I filled out the paperwork for the increase in child support and sent it in. The amount of paperwork I had to complete just to get an increase was insane. I was making it work on my own, but it was the principal of the matter. I didn't make this baby by myself. TMTSNBN owed William this.

And, for those saying they don't need the money – "I can do it myself" – do it for your child or children. It is not about you. Put that money away for his or her college or put it away, as an investment in their future. Why? Because your child is entitled to the money. The thing is you don't get to make a child and not provide for him or her. If you don't want to be a parent, then give up your rights.

I'm sure there are a lot of men, who will take care of a child, who is not biologically theirs. Thankfully, this is what "TMTSNBN" eventually did – he gave up his rights to William. This allowed my husband, Marcus LaCroix, to adopt William.

But, before "TMTSNBN" gave up his rights, the child support enforcement office wanted to know everything about "our situation" - down to how much I was paying for insurance. I was like why? Is he going to pay half? But, I did what they asked and sent the information into the office.

After mailing the paperwork, I called the Child

Support Enforcement Office (CSEO) to follow-up. When she called me back, she stated she never received my paperwork. And, on top of that, she was nasty to me. She was so nasty that it felt like she thought she was doing *me* a favor by even answering the phone. It's almost like she felt the people getting child support were somehow beneath her. I went off and I mean I went off.

See, at the time, I was *still* battling depression, abandonment, and a semi-ex-husband (who decided to marry someone else, while we were *still* married) issues. I was also going to school, working full-time, doing my best to take care of William, while trying to heal myself from the damage I had experienced.

So, after I went off on her, I hung up in her face. Was I wrong? Yes. But, she deserved it in my mind.

I then requested a new caseworker and re-sent the paperwork. Again, it was about William and what was rightfully owed to him. I sent her a copy of the same documents and a few weeks later, she called me back and told me she had received the paperwork.

That call was pleasant.

I got a court date but had to miss a day of work because the courthouse was Conway, SC. I lived in Columbia, SC. I got there early and had to wait. He, on the other hand, *never* showed up. So, with tears in my eyes, I drove back to Columbia. I was mad that I had missed work. I was mad that I had wasted my time. I was mad that William wouldn't receive his increase in child support or any payment at all.

As I was driving home, Tiffany, my sista-friend, called to ask how everything went. When I told her what happened all she said was, "Get it together because we are going to get through this together!" After that, I let it go. I *still* planned to get the increase for my son, but I refused to let it stress me out or knock me down.

I just let the missed child support payments stack up. FYI: When a parent doesn't pay his or her child support payment like he or she is supposed to, the amount increases over time. So, either way, he was going to pay.

Let's be honest, TMTSNBN was not trying to do anything. He saw William when I took him to see him and that was it. Someone once said to me that it is the mother's job to make sure her children have a relationship with their father(s). I do not agree with that concept. It is the mother's job to make sure a relationship between the child and the other parent continues – but the father must also be a willing participant.

Thankfully, I know how to not like someone and *still* work with him, especially when it comes to my child. My personal view of someone has nothing to do with you being a good parent. There are a lot of people, who can't be together, but are still good parents to their child (ren).

So, if you make a conscious effort to spend time with your child and be a part of his or her life, I am willing to do my part. So, for me, paying your child support had nothing to do with how I saw him, as a person. I didn't hold my son hostage from TMTSNBN, because he wasn't paying his child support.

And, although I refuse to "dog out" TMTSNBN, I am *still* going to tell the truth. He was hard to deal with at the time. But, William *still* had a stable home environment. I refused to put him through what I went through, as a child. I prayed that my family would be united in one house with us all having the same last name. Well, even if it didn't happen with TMTSNBN, it did eventually happen – with my husband. He adopted William and now we *all* carry the LaCroix last name.

## Homework

### *Acknowledge*

I had to acknowledge a few things, while on my "daddy journey." The truth is "I had an issue." When my grandfather died in 1997, I felt alone. I felt there was no one, who would have my back like he did. It was not until my husband and I began seeing a counselor that I realized I didn't trust anyone to do anything. I didn't think anyone would ever come through for me or do what he or she said he or she was going to do. I never got my hopes up, so when it didn't happen, I didn't feel any way about it.

On the flip side, I was also dealing with my own "daddy" *and* TMSNBN issues. Neither one of them did what they said they would do and neither one of them came through for me or William. It was these "issues" that started hurting my current marriage. I had trust issues and *still* do, to an extent. It is much better than it used to be, but I *still* don't have "expectations "(in general). And, I am *still* working through that piece.

But, because of my trust issues, I have always had a hard time letting people into my inner circle. In fact, I only have a couple of "sista-friends," and even they don't know *everything* about me. The only person that knows *everything* about me, outside of God, is my husband. So, you're getting a peek into my personal life just from reading this book.

I also acknowledge that when it came to TMTSNBN, I *chose* to be with him. And, I never spoke negatively about him in front of my son. Even when I really wanted to. It gives me peace that William can say I never swayed his judgment of his biological father in any way. William's thoughts about his biological father are based on his own experiences with him – not my personal beliefs or experiences with him.

As women, we hold grudges. We also make decisions in rage and anger. Moreover, we sometimes hurt our children by projecting our opinions onto them, not realizing that it is damaging them. We don't realize that we are not telling the entire story. That we are coming from our own perspectives. I knew William was going to have a rough time with TMTSNBN. That is why I felt I needed to step in and voice my opinion. His biological father was emotionally damaging to him.

The reason I didn't say much was because I decided to be with TMTSNBN. What does that say about me? I slept with him. And, I *chose* to sneak around and be with him. I thought we had something, but we didn't. So, when I thought about bad-mouthing him, I remembered that I put myself in that situation. And, as a result, it was on me to take full responsibility for my part in it. I had to ask myself:

~ What is your part in all of this?
~ Did you *choose* to be in this situation?
~ Do you take full responsibility in the situation?

### Address

People say, "Let it go and move on with your life" all of the time. But, how can you do that when you have never acknowledged that there is an issue that needs to be "addressed?" The only way you can alleviate something is by "addressing" it. In other words, you can't heal and be *free* of something until it has been "addressed." There are ways you can "address" an issue, for instance, you can talk to the person. Keep in mind that the person may not understand where you are coming from or what you are trying to do. He or she may not even acknowledge that there is an "issue." Just know, it is not about them. It's about your healing process. As I said before, my dad didn't apologize because he couldn't *see* that there was an "issue." Be prepared for that.

Write a letter and send it to the person or burn it. I have done both. You can even see a counselor. I have gone to one on several occasions and it helped. Talking to someone who has knowledge on this topic or who can help you get in touch with your true feelings is great. You can also take a spiritual journey or channel your energy into strengthening your spirituality. Regardless, at the end of the day, these things must be "addressed," if you expect to live your best life. It is important to find something that works for you, so you don't pass these things onto others.

**Alleviate**

After you have "acknowledged" that there is an "issue" and you have "addressed" it, it is time to decide how you are going to "alleviate" it.

- ~ Is it a place you can no longer go to?
- ~ Are these people you can no longer be around?
- ~ Do you want the relationship to continue?
- ~ Or, are you *choosing* not to participate in it anymore?
- ~ How will your decision affect others?
- ~ Will others get it?

These are the questions you need to answer to heal. The good news is you can now answer these questions from a place of peace. Some relationships I have *chosen* to maintain, while others I have *chosen* to let go. My goal now is to do what is best for me - my peace and joy. You will be ineffective if you do not love yourself enough to value yourself.

## Study Hall

---

1. What are some things I need to *acknowledge, address,* and *alleviate*?

2. List these things and describe what you need to do to accomplish each task.

# Divide & Degree

Divide /di·vide | \də-ˈvīd - To separate, to be distinct, or to be apart from one another.

Degree / de·gree | \di-ˈgrē/- A particular standing especially in regard to dignity and/or worth.

**LESSON-** "Don't allow people or things to separate you from who you should be divinely connected to."

*D*ivide and degree go hand-in-hand. I have noticed that people will attempt to put a "divide" into your relationship. Spiritually, we know that nothing can separate us from the love of God, but do we *still* hold the same value and regard in our earthly relationships?

I have found that some people make conscious attempts to separate you from your relationships.

But, many of these relationships have divine connections. These relationships do not solely consist of being married; they also include other relationships like parent-child relationships, friendships, mentorships, etc...

Let's be clear, I am *not* just talking about the relationships we *choose*. Yes, those have taught us great lessons, however, those are not *true* divine relationships. I am also *not* telling anyone to stay in toxic relationships.

I am, however, referring to the people, who have made an impact in your life. For instance, that 5th-grade teacher that reminded you of just how special you are, or that coach, who saw the potential in you - potential you never really saw in yourself. Maybe, it was a high school teacher, who took you under her wing or an employer, who helped you move up the corporate ladder. It is those relationships that have helped you grow and develop.

Friendships, relationships, and family dynamics

help you become the person you are destined to be. The truth is some relationships have helped you develop for the better and some for the worst, but regardless, they have helped shape the person you are now.

However, one day you will discover that not everyone is excited for you. Some are even jealous of you. The thing is jealousy comes in all shapes and sizes, so we may not be able to recognize it when it's right in front of us. Jealousy can also manifest in many areas of our lives *and* in the people, who surround us. So, at the end of the day, it is a desire that causes people to ruin situations, tell lies, steal, become corrupted, and "divide" others.

I first encountered this within my own family dynamic. My maternal aunt was the "divide." Growing up, I remember my mom always saying, "You will never come before my sisters. I've known them since I was a little girl." She said this all of the time.

My brothers and I couldn't even go over to my other aunt's house (her other sister), because she said we were too bad and would tear stuff up. So, as a kid, I was confused because I thought "family was everything." I was taught that you should never go against the family. But, I felt like a second-class citizen in my own family. To be honest, I think it made me protect and defend my son, William, even more, when it comes to certain situations.

Over the years, I believed that my mom's sisters put a "divide" between my mom and her children. But, the biggest "divide" was between me and my mom. It began during childhood and continued into my late twenties. *Still*, I vowed to always take care of her, no matter what.

I didn't have to vow to take care of her, but I wanted to be right with God. So, regardless of what others said about me or the things people told my mom about me, I was *still* determined to take care of her.

But, to be honest, it has gotten to the point, in

which I have consulted an attorney about harassment and deformation I have received. My aunts have said some pretty harsh things to me and about me. They have even tried to harm me. Did I engage with them? Yes, I did. Do I take full responsibility for my actions? Yes, I do. The sad part was my mother never defended me. I was always wrong and what they did to me didn't matter to her. In her eyes, they were always right.

There has also been a "divide" in my friendships and relationships. In fact, there have been times, when a relationship with one person caused me to not have a relationship with another person – because of them. Or, one of them found a way to cause confusion in my other relationships.

Thus, your commitment to a relationship determines how willing you are to fight for it. You must be very clear on your relationship's purpose, and how it will serve you in your life.

The truth is we tend to hang onto people and things that don't positively serve us. Please understand; no one should only give 50% in a relationship. I know it is common to say, "This relationship is 50/50." However, that is a false statement because that means you only have to give half of yourself and the other person only has to bring half of himself or herself. Then, you have a whole person. But, how effective is that? It is not. When you choose to give all or none of yourself to a relationship, you are basically saying, "I am either committed to you and this relationship fully or I am not."

There are also times when relationships must be completely severed. Sometimes, it's for a good reason and sometimes, it's for a bad one. But, at the end of the day, it may be the only way you receive peace. Relationships should evolve over time. They should help you grow and mature, not hold you back or cause you to regress. Others should notice a change in you, because of the relationships in your life. And, while we are on the subject of change, I want to talk about how I have changed and how my reactions have also changed.

In my relationships, I tend to put myself last to help and support others. In doing so I neglected myself. However, as I changed, I chose myself first as it allowed me to support others without it feeling like a burden. Furthermore, as I have grown, I have learned to let go of people and things who are not going in the direction I'm going.

When you are in a happy place - acquiring nice things, growing your business, having a fulfilling marriage, and traveling, but you start to think you are better than others, you have not changed. But, when you value yourself and what you bring to the table, you have changed.

To be clear, all of these things are direct reflections of how others feel about themselves – reflections that have been projected onto you. So, you need to tell yourself, "I need to believe in myself for things to get better." *You are not the problem.*

But, what I hate the most is when people say

condescending things. You know those who say things like, "You think you are better than others" or, "Must be nice!" or, "You own a business, why can't you make your own schedule?" or, "You have a husband, so of course, you can travel." Or, "You don't have time for me anymore…" or, "You never come to visit anymore." And, my favorite, "I haven't seen you in a while…"

I get so caught up in these comments that I often find myself saying the same thing to others, explaining myself, or second-guessing my decisions. But, I now realize that I need to take a stand and re-evaluate my relationships. I have also found that I must make a conscious *choice* to be happy and *allow* the joy of the Lord to be my strength.

There are levels to relationships because everyone cannot get a front-row seat to the story of your life. Compare your life to a theatre. Your life consists of front-row seats, back row/rear seats, and balcony seats.

The people, who sit in the front-row, are the most important to you. They are the ones, who play an active role in your life. You value them because they support and understand you. You don't need to speak to them every day, but they know what you need and you know what they need. There is a strong bond built in these relationships.

The people, who sit in the rear seats, want to see the show, but don't want to see you be successful. Sometimes, we have to give certain people in our lives rear seats. These people want to say they are "present" in our lives, but only "show up" every once in a while. The truth is they just don't want to miss anything - especially not an opportunity to tell others "what happened." You may be "friendly" with these individuals, but you are very cautious about what you tell them. Because they usually have ulterior motives. In other words, they "show up" for a reason – a reason that could be good or bad. But, their ultimate goal is to exaggerate things and stir up drama.

Lastly, there are those in the balcony seats. You can *still* see the stage from the balcony, even if others call this area the "Peanut Gallery." You may know these individuals, or you may not. The best part is you really don't care too much about their opinion.

Some of these individuals may follow you on social media, but if you tell them about your dreams and goals, all you hear is crickets.

Then, there are those balcony people, who think they know you based on what they heard from others or what they saw on your social media pages. Their judgment is not based on fact and experience rather, it is pure assumption.

My "sista-friends" and I are committed to telling each other what we need from each other. We spend time together occasionally; however, we also make an effort to speak with each other weekly.

So, if they don't hear from me within 7-days, someone comes to my house to check on me, face -

times me on my phone, or asks my husband where I am. Truthfully, I wouldn't have it any other way. It works for us. We don't have to talk to or see each other every day, but I *still* know what is happening with them and vice versa. Therefore, my "sista-friends" are front row seaters.

Where do people sit in your life? Don't just think about this question from a theatrical perspective – also think about it from a biblical perspective. The Bible talks about the *Outer Courts*, *Inner Court*, and *Holys of Holys*. Thus, I have "divided" my relationships in the same manner. The *Outer Court* consists of people who really don't know me.

I would call then "associates." These individuals know me…somewhat. In other words, they only know me through an event or business deal. They may have seen my booth or spoken with me, but they don't have an in-depth relationship with me. Even those who have done business with me, *still* only know a surface version of who I am.

My *Inner Court* consists of my causal friends. This also includes a few people, who go to church with me. They know me personally and professionally. We catch up from time-to-time. Some have been demoted from my *Holys of Holys*, but we are still cool. I share just enough, hang out just enough, talk just enough business, and know just enough of basic things about their family.

I consider my *Holys of Holys* my family. The thing is 90% of these people are not even blood relatives. But, to me, they are my *family*. I call them "sister," "brother," "auntie," "mom," etc. We are extremely close. For example, my sister in Virginia was there for me when one of my maternal aunts threw me out of my grandmother's (she was deceased at the time) home. She was also there for me when my maternal aunt came to my job and made a scene. It was the worst experience of my life.

And, my sister in Columbia was there for me when I had a miscarriage. She gave me a shoulder to cry on - no questions asked! This sister even came to my house to make sure my family was taken care of, while I was in the hospital.

My point is, it is important to know where people fit into your life. It is equally important not to force them into areas of your life they don't belong in. Seek the Lord for guidance, because there were times I didn't do that, and as a result, some of my relationships negatively affected me.

**Homework**

*Acumen*

Create a list of the relationships you have and of the ones you are on the verge of letting go. Also list those, who are in positions they shouldn't be in. Pray about these individuals. Ask God to peacefully remove people from your life, if they are not supposed to be there. This mentality has saved me from serious heartbreak in the past.

Also, keep in mind that just because your relationship is not like it used to be, it does not mean there is an "issue." In fact, it could just mean that the dynamic has changed. This will allow you to "acumen," or make good decisions when it comes to your relationships.

**Assure**

Don't allow others to "divide" your relationships. I have encountered this more, as a mother, than anywhere else. Some people tend to be jealous of certain dynamics. I was once one of those people. I didn't try to break people up, but I did attempt to change people to fit my perception and "expectations."

The truth is having a *real* relationship with someone takes time and effort, but if it is important to you, you have to be willing to accept the person for who he or she is – not who you want him or her to be. When you don't know how to foster great relationships, because you've never experienced them, you are more likely to sabotage the ones you have out of ignorance.

For example, in the past, my relationship with one of my closest friends fell apart. It even got to the point where we were at war with each other.

But, even though we were not friends anymore, I vowed to never divulge anything she told me because she was *still* important to me.

And, after a few years, we were able to mend our broken friendship. And, now we are closer than ever. So, even though I loved her dearly, I had to let her go until the time was right to resume our friendship. So, as you can see, sometimes we need to break away from the people we love, so we can grow and come back together.

### Study Hall

1. How many relationships have you held onto…relationships you should have let go a long time ago? Why did you hold onto them?

2. Has someone "divided" your relationships? Who? And, how have you dealt with this "divide" and the "divider?"

3. How are you redefining your relationships now?

# *Deal-Breakers*

Deal-breaker / deal-break·er (Noun) - A factor or issue that if left unresolved, during negotiations, could cause one party to withdraw from the deal.

**LESSON** – "Stick to your guns, because it matters."

or those of you, who probably did not read my bio or the Foreward, I own a business called, "The LaCroix Agency." We serve entrepreneurs, professionals, and non-profits (mostly churches) in the area of event and talent management. We also assist with live events and handle other management services, such as speaking engagements, venue negotiations, vendor opportunities, etc.

I decided to go into the hospitality industry

through event and talent management, because I wanted to serve others. I also believe people need tangible tools to help them win. Through event and talent management, we connect with potential clients who do this very thing. We are very clear about what we do and how we can serve others. We know what needs to be done to best serve our clients. But, more importantly, we know our limits.

We all have limits. Or, as some would call it, *boundaries*. We should include these limits (boundaries) in both our personal and business lives. The truth is there are things you can't and will not tolerate. I've found over the years, when I didn't maintain limits or when I didn't say, "This is a 'deal-breaker'" or "This goes against my ethics and morals," devastating things happened. If you go against your moral compass, once the ball starts rolling there is no stopping it.

These types of "deal-breakers" caused me to lose a piece of myself. And, once you start losing pieces of yourself, you are on your way to rock bottom.

I experienced most "deal-breakers" in my relationships. I learned that we determine how others treat us. How? Because we are the ones that set limits, boundaries, and "deal-breakers" in the first place.

In other words, the moment you *allow* something to slide, you *allow* others to treat you how they see fit. So, in most cases, it is really about your tolerance. Have you ever heard the saying, "I'm drawing a line in the sand?" Well, it's not really a line in the sand, because you have allowed others to cross it without stopping them. You haven't said to them, "You're not going to do this to me!" What you need to say to them is, "You are not going to make me feel less than. You are not going to make me feel unappreciated, unloved, disrespected, judged, etc."

We must establish these "deal-breakers," when we communicate with others. Because if we say it's ok this one time, then we are ultimately opening the door for them to break our "deal-breakers" over and over again. I can't tolerate people who talk to me as though I am beneath them. I've had it happen to me many times – from my ex-husband to my family members. Because of this, I often ask myself three vital questions: (1) Is this person worth fighting for? Meaning, do I value this relationship enough to try again or keep trying and (2) Is the argument so big that we can't make a 'comeback?' In other words, is it impossible for us to ever be friends again? And, (3) Am I willing to forgive the betrayal, deception, mean words, discouragement, etc., and just let it all go?

For example, my "sista-friend" and I once had a knockdown drag-out argument. It was so bad that I told her that I would leave her and just pick up her children on the side of the road if I saw them and they needed help. That's how mad I was.

I won't go into details about what happened, but I was furious. She was mad too and probably just as mad as me – or madder. However, even though we were mad at each other, she *still* came to one of my events. So, for three days, while she was attending the event, I had to be the "professional Martisha LaCroix." In other words, I had to put my anger aside, even though I wanted to fight her and during most of the event, I wanted to punch her in her face.

It wasn't apparent that we had an "issue" with each other, and I didn't want everyone else in our "business," so I stayed calm. The truth is I had something to lose if I acted "out of character" there. If you want to last in the business industry, you have to learn how to manage your emotions – even when you don't want to.

I had to learn that the hard way. But, there are *still* times when I make mistakes in this area. In these situations, you must know what to do, when to do it, and how to do it.

If you are wondering what changed things between us...Well, people we both knew passed away suddenly, causing her to ask me, "If we died today, do you think we would die *still* mad at each other?" I responded with, "Yes, because I feel like you owe me an apology." That one statement turned into a three-hour conversation of what was actually a misunderstanding.

The lesson learned from this experience is that it is important to communicate one's boundaries within a relationship. In the case of me and my "sista-friend," *both* needed to clarify the boundaries in our relationship. We also needed to discuss the boundaries that were crossed and how we could move forward together.

If we never got the chance to "bounce back" from the conflict, we wouldn't be where we are now. Because we clarified our boundaries, we were able to move forward with our relationship.

It is common to want to stay mad. I get it. I also want to stay mad. However, it's not healthy to stay mad. If you do that, all of your friendships and relationships will fail. There are two reasons why people stay mad.

First, it is easier for us to hold grudges than communicate. It's easier for us to continue to "be hurt," than forgive one another and move on. Why is that? Because some of us view forgiveness as a sign of "weakness."

When someone hurts us in the worst way possible, we believe forgiving that person means we condone their actions – when we don't. So, we refuse to forgive him or her. This mentality couldn't be further from the truth. We actually get *stronger*, as people, when we forgive, let things go, and move on with our lives.

This makes us *stronger* because we prevent what could become a "divide" and a destroying of our relationships – our *real* relationships. The relationships that make a positive impact on our lives. Don't get me wrong, some relationships *need* to be destroyed, but I'm referring to relationships that are important for our growth and cultivation.

Secondly, we stay mad because we *choose* not to let the issue go. We hold onto the issue, so we can justify our actions. It provides us with something to talk about and argue about. It gives us a reason to keep the drama going. It also gives us a reason to be *mad*.

The same mentality can be applied to our "deal-breakers." If a relationship is valuable to you, you need to communicate what hurt you and what boundaries were crossed. Then, you need to listen to the other person's perspective, as well and evaluate the following:

~ What are your "deal-breakers?"

~ What is stopping you from having a productive relationship?

~ What is going to make you say, "This relationship is *not* worth it?

~ What is it going to take for you to say, "I'm setting boundaries? I'm not drawing lines in the sand anymore, but drawing concrete lines, because I'm not tolerating broken boundaries again."

Don't look at conflict as a "bad thing," because conflict can be a "good thing" in certain situations. That is why you need to know what your "deal-breakers" are – and not abandon them.

As mentioned previously, there are times when a relationship should end. However, you can distance yourself from someone without completely ending the relationship. Two great examples of this are (1) being friends, but not being able to work together, and (2) getting divorced, but remaining co-parents.

I once had a long-standing client, who I worked with for 5-years. We completed several projects together, and in my opinion, we worked well together. However, over the years, things changed between us - something happened that I *chose* to overlook.

I never addressed the issue with him, nor did I stop working with him. The thing is, the "instances" I overlooked revolved around money. I tried to help this client and others by using the name of my business in their contracts. I never should have done that, I get it.

Did I know better? Yes, I did. Was what I did

foolish? Absolutely. Because I put my business name in the contract, I was held responsible for my clients' debt. But, this situation with my long-standing client caused drama in my marriage. Why? Mainly, because my husband is also my business partner. So, he is *always* going to have my back. Now, he may not agree with all of my decisions, but we are *still* in this together.

To put things into perspective, me and this client had both a business *and* personal relationship. I take full responsibility for blurring these lines. The crazy thing is, as I write this, I realize I have business relationships with my "sista-friends," - business relationships that have concrete guidelines.

However, in this case, I had "expectations" for my long-standing client – "expectations" I should not have had. I know you are wondering what happened. Well, a bomb went off that forced my hand.

I was accused of stealing from both of my long-standing clients because they didn't meet the minimum requirement for the number of rooms they booked at a hotel, so I told them they needed to pay what they owed. Well, as you probably guessed - that didn't go over too well with them.

We then had a meeting and that didn't go over too well either. During the meeting, I was very clear - I would no longer be doing events for them. I planned to close out their accounts at the end of the year. Note: I had previously agreed to do two more events. I had put my credibility on the line, and because of that, "The LaCroix Agency" had to pay $5,000 to the hotel to cover my clients' debts.

You're probably saying, "You are crazy! I would never have done that!" But, if you think about it, you have done something similar. Now, you may have not done something to the level that I did, but you have probably broken your own "deal-breakers" with certain people. For example, you may have given certain people deals, did things for them for free, and/or put your credibility on the line by co-signing for them.

We do these things and then turn around and get mad because others have screwed us. What do we do in retaliation? We put our "business" on Facebook (which I have never done). Guess what happens after that? We do it all over again. So, at some point, we have to say to ourselves, "Enough is enough!"

The situation with my clients really took a toll on me - mentally, emotionally, and physically. The truth is, it broke my confidence! It was killing my love for the business!

The only thing that kept me afloat was sitting in my prayer chair and asking the Lord what I should do to keep moving forward. But, He didn't say anything - at first. Then, He answered me. He told me to go back, keep working the business, and try again.

Now, I'm pretty sure He didn't mean for me to try again with those same clients. I think He meant for me to try again with new clients. I then asked Him, "Lord, do you not see that I am being made a fool of?" I laugh now, but I *still* have those moments with God from time-to-time.

If my husband didn't already know me so well, he'd think I'd gone crazy, when I shared these conversations with him. The more I talked, the more I cried. The more I cried, the more He reminded me of what a tough cookie I am. During this time, I was being rebuilt. So, I continued to go to conferences, and I continued to meet new people – people, who wanted to work with me. I met new people, who said, "I heard about you!"

I even turned down business opportunities because they didn't line-up with what God said to me. In fact, by the time you read this, I will have released other positions from my business that did *not* align with what God has called me to do. Why am I doing this? Well, because I recognize my purpose and know my "deal-breakers."

My fee is my fee and I am worth every penny of it. Plus, I have learned that I can't *allow* anyone to devalue me and what I know is my value.

I am *free*. *Free* to be me. And, *free* to do things my way (God's way).

## Homework

### *Articulate*

Voice your concerns, "deal-breakers," opinions, and reasoning. Be clear on what you will tolerate and what you will not tolerate. Don't allow anyone to hold you hostage to his or her opinion, negativity, and/or toxicity. Say what you have to say without being disrespectful and give yourself the *freedom* to express yourself without anyone making you feel inadequate or "less than." If the relationship is meant to work out, it will work.

### *Advance*

I know this may not be the word you are looking for, but you have to "advance" yourself. This involves letting some things go. It is important to understand that "letting things go," doesn't mean you have to rekindle an unhealthy relationship. You just need to be in a space to be healed.

So, stop *allowing* the past to hold you back.

Don't *allow* hurt feelings to take you to a place, where you make excuses, as to why you are so mean and nasty to others. Don't make excuses, as to why you're unable to do what you need to do. "Advance" yourself by *freeing* yourself of your past decisions. And lastly, stop mishandling yourself and stop *allowing* others to mishandle you, as well.

### Study Hall

1. How have you handled "deal-breakers" in the past?
2. Did that work out in your best interest?
3. In what areas do you need to set boundaries?
4. What boundaries are you putting in place?

# Dead Weight

Dead Weight/ˈded ˈˌwāt/ (Noun)-A heavy or oppressive burden.

**LESSON-** "Let it go before you drown and take others with you."

I used to think it was only past experiences or relationships that could be considered "dead weight." But, I have come to realize, it is much more than that.

Imagine a large ship with an anchor. When the captain wants the ship to stay in one place, he releases the anchor. The anchor then goes to the bottom of the ocean, preventing the ship from drifting away. Now, imagine how long the chain has to be for the anchor to reach the ocean floor.

In retrospect, the size of the anchor doesn't

compare to the size of the ship. Now, Google images of a ship and anchor. The anchor probably isn't even an eighth of the size of the ship, let alone a fourth of it. Yet, it can *still* hold this huge ship in place.

That, my friends, is what we call "dead weight." This type of weight holds you still, so you can't move forward in your life.

I had a lot of "dead weight" in my life because I *chose* to. Have you ever heard someone say, "You are holding me back and keeping me from accomplishing something?" Or, "You're doing this or that to me..." The truth is no one is doing anything to you.

In other words, you have *chosen* to stick with a person or stay in a situation, circumstance, or relationship that has become "dead weight" to you. This "dead weight" is killing you. More specifically, you're at a standstill and can't move forward. You are *allowing* these people, places, and things to control you. You have to let this "dead weight" go because it is killing you spiritually, emotionally, physically, and mentally.

I held onto people too long with the hope that things would change. I thought certain people in my life would "get it together" and "do better." I used to believe that those people would change because they loved me. They are going to treat me better, right? They are going to do right by me, right? Well, as I tell young children, "That is a No-No!"

I was the one who had to change for there to be any change in my life. People were either going to support my business – or they were not. That was my biggest hurdle to get over.

Let me *free* you…

Are you ready? Here it is, the people you think are going to support you - are not. That is inclusive of, but not limited to your friends, family, church, co-workers, "baby daddies," spouse, social media followers, and anyone else I neglected to mention.

The problem is you are looking for validation. You want someone to acknowledge what you are doing. That is why you do things for free or charge the bare minimum – even though you know that it won't feed your family or make you proud of yourself. You justify your actions by saying, "I am just in the beginning stages" or "They are my friends, so it's ok."

Now, let's be clear, I do things for my "sista-friends," even though I might not get paid. However, these women have businesses of their own, so it is more like a barter than a "handout." But, I don't do that with everyone.

Back to my point, most of my friends are not my clients. As a result, I don't expect them to purchase my products or even come to my events. I know this is going to anger some people, but even those in my "church family" are not my clients. What does that mean? It means I don't expect them to purchase my products either, although some might. Will I provide them with services? Maybe or maybe not.

Just because you go to church with someone,

doesn't mean you have to give them things for free or for a discounted rate. But, some church members think you should be "Godly" and give them things for free. I could quote Bible scriptures right now, but I won't do that. However, what I will say is this - the church is a great place to discover your purpose and address kinks *before* talking to potential clients. The thing is, God didn't give you gifts and talents only to have them confined to four walls of a building. No, God wants you to go out, surrounded by His presence and glory to impact his entire kingdom.

Remember, the vision God gave you - the one that others may not agree with or understand. Trust me, you will still "mess up" – i.e. waste time and resources; trying to get others to understand and approve of your vision. When that happens, you'll have to go alone or do it without support. But, you'll *still* "expect" others, because you have given all of yourself to them and their projects. Because of this, you'll "expect" them to support you and cheer you on. But, the truth is, the opposite may happen. In other words, you may not receive the support and approval you desire.

You may believe you are doing great things, however, your family members, church members, and even some friends may not support you.

It is exciting to start something – i.e. a non-profit, ministry, new job, or even a new project. It is also normal to "expect" others to support you. So, what do you do? You tell these people about your hopes, dreams, plans, and progress. What happens next? You receive "dead weight" in return. The people you thought would support don't *see* what you *see.* Instead, they project their fears onto you. They don't understand your vision and mission. They simply want you to do what they want you to do. They tell you that they don't think it is a good idea. And, they ask you why you didn't do it this way or that way. The result? You end up not doing anything at all. You end up doubting yourself.

So, what do you do? You charge less than you

normally would when they tell you that your fee is too much for them to afford. This causes you to doubt yourself, and as a result, you start to think you should have stayed at your previous job because this "business thing" just isn't working. And, you experience the "fear factor." You second-guess what you have started. As a result, you start to question if the thing you want to do is going to work. You also refuse help and support from others. But, my question is why would you want people, who don't support you around anyway? What sense does that make?

It is this "dead weight" that is slowly killing us. It is killing us physically and spiritually. So, why are you not as invested in you, as you would like to be? It took me a while to learn this lesson. The "dead weight" weighed me down, because I did not believe that I was "good enough." This was especially true when I tried and failed.

It was during these times that I decided not to put myself out there and be made a fool of again. I did this because I felt it didn't work when I gave all of myself to someone or something.

I once hosted an event called "Let's Get Connected." I honestly don't want to bring it back. However, the Lord instructed me *to* bring it back. Don't judge. I have asked the Lord for forgiveness for my disobedience.

I have neglected to bring it back in the past, because of what I have gone through with the event. This event caused me to lose my money, purpose, self-esteem, and self-confidence.

By the time this book hits the shelves, you will see the "Let's Get Connected" event on the calendar again, primarily because I am in a different headspace now. Thus, I have decided to use this event to give people tangible tools that will help them win in all areas of their lives.

I have also invited people to come to this event, so they can share their expertise with others. The thing is everything I do strategically connects people with what they need to effectively do what they have been called to do.

I want people to be exposed to *realistic* tools that they don't have to search for. I just want them to be present and receive the information. Then, I want them to go out and do the work. I believe taking the searching off the table will help individuals be more successful.

So, when we first hosted the "Let's Get Connected" event, I had a big turnout. I believe this was primarily because it was free, and people, in general, love free events. The event cost my company about $1,000, but my goal was to entice individuals to retain our services in the future. In other words, I had hoped they would return as paying clients in the future.

It was my hope that the people attending the event were as excited, as I was. Surprisingly, most of the people, who attended the event, were from my church! I was super excited about the support because I believed the majority of them would return. There was such positive energy radiating from them – that is until they had to pay for my services.

Truth-be-told, I wondered why they were so excited at first – only to "change their tunes" later. Was it the date? Was it the price? When I asked them about it, most said it was the cost. But, after much thought, I realized it wasn't them - it was me. I was doing things from a place of "expectation" and not a place of "appreciation."

I was holding people to the same standard I held myself to. But, that was unfair to both me and them. I had to let the "dead weight" go.

I now have people around me who truly support me. Sometimes, they show up and sometimes, they don't and that's ok. Their energy tells me that they want me to be successful. So, even if they don't need my services or products, they *still* want me to win.

So, pin (yes, I mean thumbtack it, so you can remember what I say) this on your wall right now, stop getting upset when the people you want to support you - don't. The problem is we want certain people to "celebrate" us. Some of us also have a habit of abandoning the people, who actually want to see us win, for the one person, who don't even understand what we are doing or where we are trying to go. Then, we are let down because we put all of our energy into trying to get that one person to support us. We dismiss the people, who want to see us win for nothing. Remember, you can only please one master. So, you have two choices - to serve man or to serve God. You can't do both. You have to *choose* one and stick with it.

You can't go through life trying to make everyone happy or you will be miserable. Your focus should be on your happiness. Once you do that, you can help others do the same. God has never turned His back on me or disappointed me, so I know who I am going to *choose*.

I apologize if that offended anyone, but I have to speak my "truth." Our dreams and goals are dying from "dead weight." We continue to seek the approval of people, who have nothing to show for their own lives and who are projecting their fears and trials on us. We are *still* out here, proclaiming our faith, but not trusting God's plan for our lives. Some of us won't even *try* to do things, because others are telling us not to.

Well, the last time I checked, God is one of faith and work. These things go hand-and-hand, so regardless of what you say or do, you really aren't doing *anything* if you are not working your faith. Then, you get mad at yourself and others because of your actions – or lack thereof.

So, don't waste your time trying to sell a great idea to others. Don't focus on those, who want to know why you are doing what you are doing, why you need their support, etc. The truth is they are just weighing you down.

Thankfully, I am now back-on-track. And, I am forever grateful to the people, who have supported me. To my "riders" (you know who you are) I love you for loving me. I no longer have "expectations," and for that, I am grateful.

I commented to someone about not being concerned, if certain people don't show up or support me on special days. Then, the person I was speaking with became offended by my comment. She responded with, "Well, people care about you and want to support you." I then responded with, "Well, I think you misunderstood what I said. What I mean is that it will be great if people show up, but I will understand if they don't. But, I refuse to base my happiness or self-worth on whether they show up or not."

You see, God has brought me through a lot. He has always come through for me. So, even if others don't show up for me – I know God always will. So, let go of your "dead weight." And, don't *allow* others to dictate how you feel about yourself. Stop *allowing* others to have that type of control over you.

Remember, you are bold, brilliant, and brave – regardless of whether or not others show up or not.

You have already been defined by your Creator. So, what others say and do should have no bearing on how you feel about yourself or what you do.

Let me make this clear because someone is going to say, "Are you trying to say that church people aren't supportive?" No, that is not what I'm saying. What I am saying is don't "expect" others, including church people, to support you. Period. Also, don't think that just because you have "fellowshipped" with people at church, they will automatically support you, because you may be disappointed. Mainly, because you are holding on to false "expectation," when you should be walking in "appreciation." God has chosen me to walk out His vision for me, my attendees, my clients, and for my events. So, I am not worried about what other people did or did not do. That is in the past. My focus right now is on my current tasks.

I still "celebrate," those, who show up at my events. But, I had to stop carrying the "dead weight" of people, my past, etc. who don't. There are over seven billion people in the world, so there are people, who know what you need and people, who have what you need to be successful. So, stop depending on others to validate the vision you've been given because if you continue to do this, you will fail.

Let go of the "dead weight."

Everyone is not going to *see* or understand your vision – not your business vision - not your marriage vision - not your career vision - not any vision. So, stop wasting your time trying to get them to *see* what you *see* because it won't work.

Stop getting mad at others and stop holding onto people, who don't want to be a part of your vision. Moreover, stop holding onto people, who aren't going where you are going. *Let it all go.* Don't do it for them – do it for yourself. For your growth and development. *Let it all go.*

Your ship can't move with your anchor pinning it down. The "dead weight" of disappointment, hurt, misunderstandings, grudges, false security, guilt, self-sabotage, and abandonment are the anchors that are holding you in place and preventing you from progressing and reaching your true potential.

Freeing myself from all of that was the best thing I could have done for myself.

Thank you to my publisher, *Sanders Publications*, because without you, this would have continued to be "just a title and an idea." You pushed me to make my dream come true.

I also want to point out that "dead weight" caused me to hold onto things that weren't good for me. "Dead weight" caused me to *allow* others to kill my dreams. So, I stopped telling certain people certain things.

"Dead weight" caused me to *not* believe in myself. It also caused me to *allow* people to "take me down." "Dead weight" caused me to believe people when they told me "I wasn't good enough."

"Dead weight" also caused me to contemplate killing myself. It was the "dead weight" that caused me to do all of these things.

Furthermore, "dead weight" caused me to not feel pretty because someone told me I was ugly. Truthfully, "dead weight" also caused me to make poor decisions and hurt other people.

Because of this "dead weight," I couldn't progress in my life. Honestly, the "things" that hurt the most have the most effect on you. Those, who say it doesn't hurt, are lying. If you have ever received a spanking, you remember them far less, than the words the "spanker" said to you.

I was told, to my face, in front of other people to "rot in hell." Facts. It was by the same person, who preceded the comment with "family should stick together" and "family is *everything*." These comments came from one of my maternal aunts - in front of a room full of people. It had happened before, but that was the last time. I was done. It was hard to let it go, but I did it.

I was not appreciating and accepting who I was. Rather, I was holding onto situations that were killing me from the inside out. The other people aren't dying, but you are. Remember, you have *nothing* to prove to anyone. The thing is, letting it all go doesn't mean you approve of what someone else did, it just means you don't want to be held hostage by their actions anymore.

So, when someone says something crazy to you - say something crazy back to them. Someone once said to me, "It must be nice to buy a new car." I, in turn, responded with, "It is. God has shown favor on me." This shuts the person all the way up. I'm not going to discredit the blessings in my life to make others "feel good" about themselves. I'm also not going to *allow* others to make me feel unworthy. But, what I am going to do is let go of the "dead weight" that's holding me back from being my greatest self. *Be authentically you.* Stop trying to be what everyone wants you to be. When I let the "dead weight" go it felt like a weight had been lifted off my shoulders. I had been trying to hide the parts of me I truly liked because they didn't fit into the nice and neat box that others deemed appropriate. It was like I was living a secret life.

I told the "The Martisha Experience Group" that I love the Lord *and* trap music, and they thought that was so funny. But, it is the truth. I really do have a variety of music on my iPod and I'm not ashamed of that. It doesn't mean something is wrong with me. I have learned that it is ok to be unapologetically me.

So, let go of pleasing others because you're not a cookie-cutter person. But, know that someone is *not* going to be happy with you. So, focus on making yourself happy, regardless of what other people think, say, or do.

### Homework

*Break free of Bondage*

You must understand that "dead weight" is a form of "bondage." It keeps you in one place - doing nothing because you have not dealt with your "issues."

As a result, you are a hostage in your own life. You may not even recognize yourself anymore. So, do yourself a favor and write out what you will and will not do. Then, sign the list, as a symbol of your commitment *not* to go back to your old ways. The truth is yesterday is gone, so live in today, and plan for the future.

### Release the Baggage

Erika Badu came out with a song called, "Bag Lady." When you really listen to the lyrics, it dawns on you how "baggage" really weighs you down emotionally, physically, and spiritually. When you get a chance look up the song lyrics, it will help you *see* how "baggage" slows you down and causes you to "miss out" on *real* opportunities. Your "baggage" is not just people, places, and things; it is also your mindset. So, if you change your mindset, you'll also change your life. A positive mentality can move mountains. So, think of yourself as a royal priesthood, God's favorite, God's daughter or son, a millionaire, a great wife or husband, a great mom or dad, and/or a business owner. Also, think of yourself as powerful, defying all the odds and setting new standards. Is it a game-changer? Yes. You can change things to fit you, but with a positive mindset, you can change the game altogether. So, look through your "baggage" and call it by its name. Acknowledge that you have been carrying around "baggage" that doesn't serve your true divine purpose. Then, find something positive to replace it with. After that? Discard the "baggage," so you feel lighter and can walk in purpose.

### Study Hall

1. What are some things that have kept you bound - things you did not even realize were keeping you from progressing?
2. What "baggage" are you carrying around – baggage you need to let go of?
3. What is your plan of action for discarding this "baggage?"

# Deserve

De·serve /dəˈzərv/ (Verb) - Do something or showing qualities worthy of reward or punishment.

**LESSON** – "Thankfully, I didn't always get what I deserved. I am also thankful that God looked beyond my mistakes and errors and blessed me anyway."

Do you feel that you "deserve" happiness? Do you feel whole? Do you feel *free* and prosperous? Are you living your "best life?" Or, do you believe that because you have made bad decisions, hurt others, and/or had a rough childhood, you don't "deserve" to be happy?

Well, about a year ago, someone asked me if I felt that I married too soon. She also asked me if I thought that marrying my current husband was due to my will or God's will. I honestly responded with,

"No, I don't feel like I married too soon, and I believe it was God's will."

It is important to understand that when I met Marcus (my husband); I had already decided he was *not* the "one" for me. It wasn't because he was a terrible person, rather it was because I was in a different headspace than him, spiritually, or so I thought.

I was also at a point in my life, where I was open to *maybe* getting married again. But, what really brought us together was our friendship and William. I *still* wasn't sure, at that time; I "deserved" to have a great husband and life.

To be honest, I have self-sabotaged a lot of great things in my life. And, at the time, I was fully aware of all of the things I'd done - all of the places I'd gone - all of the things I had said - and all of the people I had hurt. That is why I didn't believe I "deserved" to be happy and blessed. I had genuinely apologized to everyone I had hurt and disappointed over the years by this time, but it didn't change how

I felt.

I had prayed that the people I hurt would forgive me (the broken me) for what I did because I really didn't know how to live right.

God reminds me that it's not that I "deserve" it, rather it is because His grace has given it unto me. That is why I consider my marriage a gift.

A particular congresswoman always comes to mind when I think about my current place in life. She once said, "I'm re-claiming my time." So, that is what I'm doing - reclaiming my time and restoring the things that were taken from me or damaged.

This is the fun part; I gain a greater "appreciation" because of it. I'm so grateful for my grace, favor, and faith. I'm also so grateful for this life I get to live. Now, I can enjoy my life without regret. But, I am most grateful to God, because He is responsible for the gifts I have received. He gets all of the credit. It may be a Higher Power or the universe for you, but for me, it's God. He has helped me desire more, "expect" more, become more, and believe more. He also made me showcase my willingness to change to receive more. He made me want to *choose* myself. People think that *choosing* yourself is selfish, and it is to a certain extent.

Think about it this way – if you are unable or unwilling to *choose* yourself, how on earth can you help someone else? So, I *choose* me - not what others want me to be and not what others want me to do. Rather, I *choose* to make strategic choices that line-up with what God has planned for me.

Not everyone is going to accept this from me, but it is what it is. The problem is many of us want more, but we are *not* willing to change to get more. It doesn't work that way.

If you decide to make changes, don't allow anyone to tell you that you don't "deserve" better because of your past – because you do. The key is opening your heart, receiving your blessings, and giving back to others. Having more means being willing to give more.

When God gives you more, it is up to you to receive those blessings and "pay it back" to others. I was "broken" before, but I did not know it. And, because of my "brokenness," I "broke" other people and *allowed* others to "break me." During this time, I began to question the very things I believed in.

~ Do I "deserve" to be a millionaire?

~ Do I "deserve" this job?

~ Do I "deserve" a fancy car?

~ Do I "deserve" to live in a nice home in a nice neighborhood?

~ Do I "deserve" to help people?

~ Do I "deserve" to serve people?

~ Do I "deserve" to live this life?

God said to me, "Yes, you do because you are a child of the King." And that was all I needed to know.

I then began to re-evaluate my conversations with myself and other people - even when I didn't *feel* or *see* anything changing. The "earning it" concept was also challenging for me – the belief that I didn't "deserve" things because I didn't work hard enough for them. However, once I understood that grace is freely given to the believer and that I had "access" to the King (God); "earning it" didn't matter anymore. I learned that "favor is not always fair."

Think about it like this – your children don't always receive things because they "earned" them. They have received some things, simply because they have "access" to you (their parents).

Do you think celebrities make their children start all the way at the bottom and work up because they had to? No, they have "access" to things others may not, because of their wealthy parents.

So, as long as you know who your Father is, you will have "access" to the things you need.

In the past, I did things wrong in so many areas of my life – i.e. in my marriage and home life, in my business, and in other relationships. On top of that, I hid the blessings I received.

The truth is I have never been one to flash or flaunt the things I have. I earn a great living and my husband takes great care of me. Nevertheless, one year, my husband bought me a gold *Pandora* bracelet. After he gave it to me, I only wore it twice within the first two months of receiving it.

One day he asked me about it. He wanted to know why I was not wearing the bracelet. I told him that I didn't want to call attention to myself, have to explain it to other people, have people asking questions about it, and/or have others look at me strangely for having it.

When I think about it now - I have done the same thing with almost every gift he has given me.

*Until I was healed.*

I know how stupid that sounds. But, it was how I felt at the time.

Because of other people, I found myself questioning if I "deserved" nice things. People would say to me, "Oh, that is new… must be nice."

Or "Y'all are *ballers* now."

They downplayed the very things I was blessed to have. Then, I ended up *not* wanting to take anything new or nice around them. But, my husband straightened me out. He really made me think about the consequences of *my* decisions.

It is a blessing to not have to struggle and to be able to purchase nice things and go on nice vacations. Grant Cardone is quoted as saying "Money can't buy happiness, but poverty can't buy anything." This quote reminds me that I am blessed, and I shouldn't have to hide this fact.

Therefore, it is this "appreciation" that others can *see* in you. It is also this "appreciation" that helps others *see* themselves as "winners." But, sometimes, the residue of self-sabotage *still* "pops up." It comes in the form of *procrastination* - something I struggle with it daily. Though, some days are easier than others. God reminds me why I do what I do. I represent Him and serve His people. So, when I think, "I am not good enough," and when things look a little "cloudy," I revert back to my purpose. Then, I re-group and try again.

I'll be the first to tell you that you "deserve" all of the wonderful things God has in store for you - in all areas of your life.

> ~ *You "deserve" greatness.*
> ~ *You deserve God's best for you.*
> ~ *You do. You do. You just do.*

You just have to desire His best more than anything in the world and be willing to put in the work. Your roots have to be strong enough to handle what is coming ahead. In other words, you need to focus on the end goal. Your goals should *not* change, because of setbacks, what others say, or even your own thoughts.

My goal is to produce prayer warriors, worshipers, faith fighters, wealth gainers, "game-changers," and "difference makers." I want my legacy to be helping others. Because they "deserve" it too.

## Homage

*Bequeath*

You must be a giver in three major areas of your life; time, talent, and treasure. Giving and receiving go hand-and-hand. Giving involves more than just giving money. I know we focus on that most, but it is *not* the only way to give. Giving your time and talent is more valuable. So, be willing to give freely without requiring anything in return. I know this can be challenging, especially if you are also in need. But, think about ways you can give to others. Be creative, and deliberately seek those who need help.

*Believe*

Believing is super important. You are more likely to act if you "believe." Do you "believe" in the very life you are trying to sell to others? Put your vision on a board and go back to it, when you experience self-doubt. Visualize having a good life, then take steps to achieve your goals. What are your short-term and long-term goals? This is important when you are trying to make a difference in someone else's life.

## Study Hall

1. List ways you can freely and openly "give" your time, talent, and treasures to others. Set a goal to complete at least one thing, in each category, within 3 months.

2. What are some things you "believe in?" Why? List three action items that are a part of your belief system.